SOLO Taxonomy in the Social Sciences

Strategies for social inquiry

Pam Hook and Craig Perry

Title:	SOLO Taxonomy in the Social Sciences Strategies for social inquiry
Authors:	Pam Hook and Craig Perry
Editor:	Tanya Tremewan
Designer:	Diane Williams
Book code:	5936
ISBN:	978-1-77655-224-5
Published:	2016
Publisher:	Essential Resources Educational Publishers Limited

United Kingdom:	Australia:	New Zealand:
Units 8–10 Parkside	PO Box 906	PO Box 5036
Shortgate Lane	Strawberry Hills	Invercargill
Laughton BN8 6DG	NSW 2012	
ph: 0845 3636 147	ph: 1800 005 068	ph: 0800 087 376
fax: 0845 3636 148	fax: 1800 981 213	fax: 0800 937 825

Websites: www.essentialresourcesuk.com
www.essentialresources.com.au
www.essentialresources.co.nz

Copyright: Text: © Pam Hook and Craig Perry, 2016
Edition and illustrations: © Essential Resources Educational Publishers Limited, 2016

About the authors: Pam Hook is an educational consultant (HookED Educational Consultancy, www.pamhook.com), who works with New Zealand and Australian schools to develop curricula and pedagogies for learning to learn based on SOLO Taxonomy. She has published articles on thinking, learning, e-learning and gifted education, and has written curriculum material for government and business. As well as authoring and co-authoring more than 15 books on SOLO Taxonomy (some of which have been translated into Danish), she is co-author of two science textbooks widely used in New Zealand secondary schools. She is also a popular keynote speaker at conferences.

Craig Perry has been an educator in New Zealand high schools since 2000, teaching geography and the social sciences. He has a passion for making learning visible for students so that they can become active and engaged participants in their own learning. Since meeting Pam Hook in 2006, Craig has made SOLO Taxonomy part of his teaching as a powerful framework that helps him and his students achieve this outcome. While still a classroom teacher, he has also been moving towards teaching teachers and is grateful for the opportunities he has had to present his thinking at several New Zealand conferences.

Acknowledgements: Thanks to Professor John Biggs for his encouragement and ongoing critique of our work with the classroom-based approach to using SOLO Taxonomy and to the many New Zealand, Australian and UK teachers and schools who have shared SOLO as a common language of learning with their social sciences students. Special thanks to Lincoln High School in Canterbury, New Zealand for the many examples of student learning outcomes in this book. We are especially grateful to Miriam Marshall and Rachel Meadowcroft for the SOLO reverse hexagons and values template examples.

Copyright notice:

All rights reserved. No part of this publication (with the exception of the specific pages identified below) may be reproduced, stored in a retrieval system, or transmitted in any form by any means, electronic or mechanical or by photocopying, recording or otherwise, without the prior written permission of the publisher. Copyright owners may take legal action against a person or organisation who infringes their copyright through unauthorised copying. All inquiries should be directed to the publisher at the address above.

Schools and teachers who buy this book have permission to reproduce the following pages only within their present school by photocopying, or if in digital format, by printing as well: pages 18, 30, 31, 32, 38, 39, 41, 42, 45, 46, 48, 49, 63 and 64. For further information on your copyright obligations, visit: New Zealand: www.copyright.co.nz, Australia: www.copyright.com.au, United Kingdom: www.cla.co.uk

Contents

Introduction	**4**
How can SOLO help?	5
1. An overview of SOLO Taxonomy and social inquiry	**6**
What is SOLO Taxonomy?	6
What is social inquiry?	8
How do SOLO and social inquiry work together?	9
2. Teaching approaches that enhance outcomes	**15**
Alignment and SOLO	15
Connection and SOLO	27
Community and SOLO	34
3. SOLO strategies for developing declarative knowledge	**36**
Observational thinking – description	36
Experimental thinking – causality and making inferences	40
Correlational thinking – prediction	43
Conceptual thinking – generalising	47
4. SOLO strategies for developing functioning knowledge	**55**
Interpreting resources	55
Constructing resources	57
Communication skills	58
Social skills	59
Fieldwork skills	61
5. What do students say?	**63**
Conclusions	**65**
References	**66**
Index of exhibits and templates	**67**

Introduction

SOLO makes it much easier to work because you know what the task is asking. It helped me focus on what I needed to find out and gave me clear ideas on how to write my report and speech. Year 9 student, Lincoln High School

Social scientists use social inquiry in important ways to explore social phenomena (observable occurrences involving people) that affect the quality of our everyday experience. These phenomena occur within and between families, in schools, through economies, social unrest, wars, famines, pandemics, networks, mass media and politics. In the social sciences learning area of the New Zealand Curriculum (primary and secondary), these social phenomena are categorised as:

- Identity, culture and organisation
- Place and environment
- Continuity and change
- The economic world.

The undisputed benefit of this approach for social sciences teachers is that they can apply the tools, strategies and action competencies of the social sciences discipline in various high-interest, contemporary contexts that are aligned to the lived worlds and experiences of their students. Teachers do this by continually adapting their lessons to what is current, and connecting this content to authentic contexts that pique students' curiosity and inquiry. As well as being interesting, it is work that matters because understanding the social sciences contributes directly to young people becoming skilled and active participants in an uncertain future – skilled and active participants in their own lives.

Students act and think like social scientists when they undertake social inquiry into social phenomena. As part of the United Kingdom Campaign for Social Science, Professor Audrey Ostler (2011) proposed 10 reasons why we need the social sciences (Exhibit 1). The reasons are individually and collectively persuasive and explain why it matters that students learn to think like social scientists.

Exhibit 1: Ostler's 10 reasons for studying the social sciences

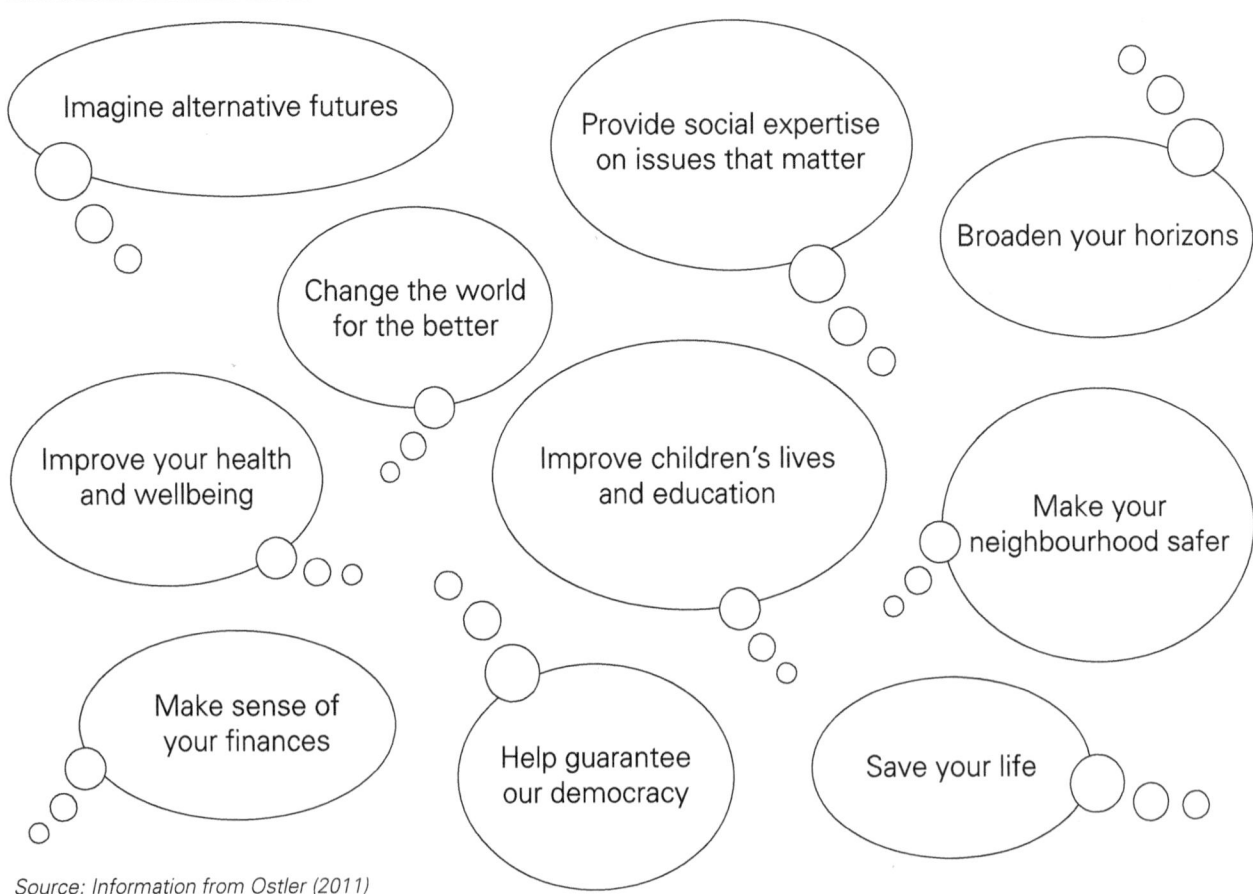

Source: Information from Ostler (2011)

How can SOLO help?

SOLO Taxonomy in the Social Sciences explores how using a model like SOLO Taxonomy can enhance students' social inquiry into significant issues. Our experience is that using SOLO Taxonomy (Biggs and Collis 1982) as a model of learning helps students think deeply throughout their social inquiry activities. For example, as Exhibit 2 illustrates, SOLO helps students with learning how to:

- **collect** quantitative and qualitative data (SOLO multistructural level – bringing in ideas)
- **analyse** data to identify causes (SOLO relational level – linking ideas)
- **predict** occurrences (SOLO extended abstract level – extend ideas)
- **develop** evidence-based intervention programmes and social action to address the social phenomena in some way (SOLO extended abstract level).

Exhibit 2: How we understand social phenomena

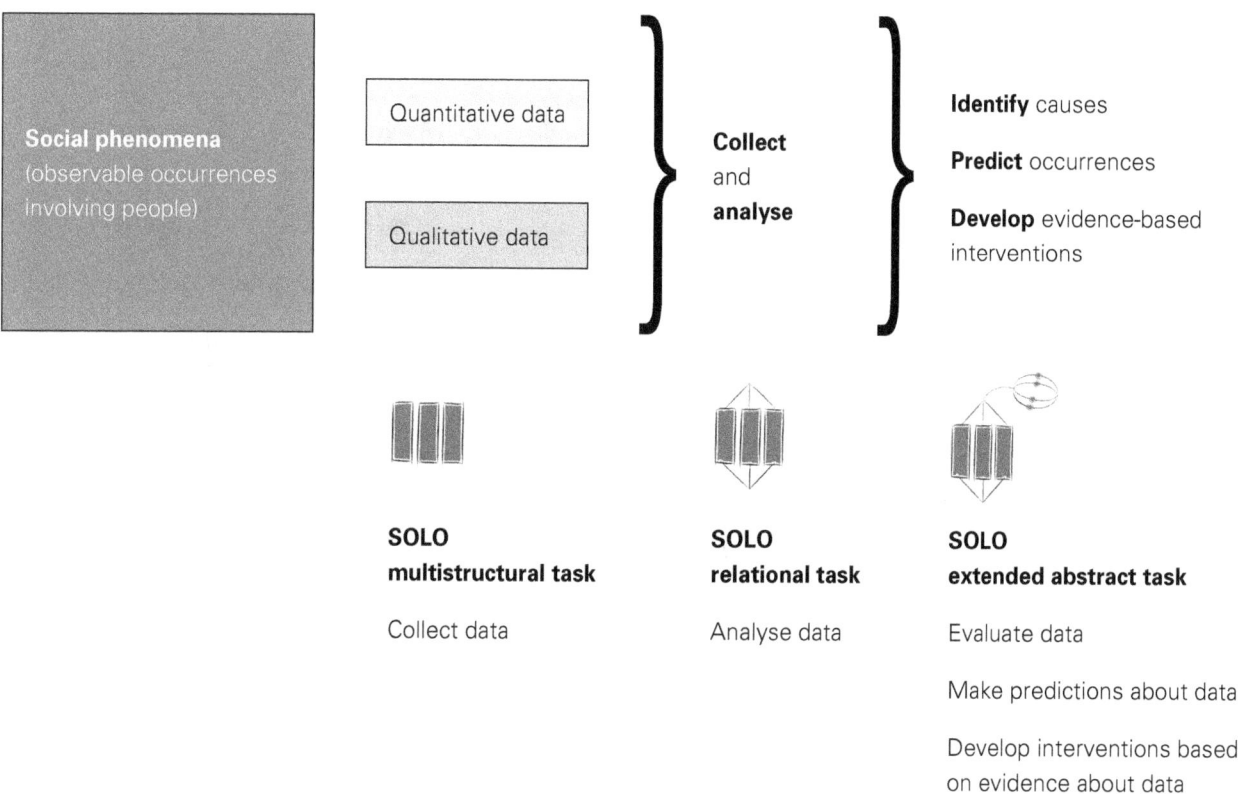

This book shares a range of student examples from Lincoln High School, New Zealand showing how students learn when they are participating in classroom-based approaches to SOLO Taxonomy in the social sciences. For further examples, see Pam Hook's HookED SOLO Taxonomy boards on Pinterest (www.pinterest.com/solotaxonomy/solo-taxonomy-in-geography and www.pinterest.com/solotaxonomy/solo-taxonomy-in-history).

1. An overview of SOLO Taxonomy and social inquiry

This section first introduces SOLO Taxonomy and social inquiry separately before exploring how the two can work together to the benefit of both tasks and outcomes in social inquiry.

What is SOLO Taxonomy?

Structure of Observed Learning Outcome (SOLO) Taxonomy is a model of learning that provides a simple, reliable and robust framework for three levels of understanding – surface, deep and conceptual (Biggs and Collis 1982). Exhibit 1.1 sets out the five-level framework.

Exhibit 1.1: SOLO levels, symbols and hand signs

Prestructural	Unistructural	Multistructural	Relational	Extended abstract
Learning outcomes show unconnected information and no organisation.	Learning outcomes show simple connections but importance is not noted.	Learning outcomes show connections are made but significance to overall meaning is missing.	Learning outcomes show connections are made and parts are synthesised with the overall meaning.	Learning outcomes go beyond the subject and make links to other concepts – generalising, predicting, evaluating.
No idea	One idea	Many ideas	Related ideas	Extended ideas

The five levels see the student's understanding progress both quantitatively and qualitatively:

- At the **prestructural** level of understanding, the student approaches the task inappropriately, and has missed the point or needs help to start.

    The next two levels, unistructural and multistructural, are associated with surface levels of understanding – bringing in information.

- At the **unistructural** level, the student picks up one aspect of the task, and their understanding is disconnected and limited. The jump to the multistructural level is quantitative.

- At the **multistructural** level, the student knows several aspects of the task but misses their relationships to each other and the whole.

    The progression to relational and extended abstract outcomes is qualitative.

- At the **relational** level, the aspects are linked and integrated, and contribute to a deeper level of understanding – and a more coherent understanding of the whole.

- At the **extended abstract** level, the student builds on their new understanding at the relational level to rethink it at another conceptual level, look at it in a new way, and use it as the basis for prediction, generalisation, reflection, or creation of new understanding (Hook and Mills 2011) (Exhibit 1.2).

Exhibit 1.2: Higher-order thinking and SOLO Taxonomy

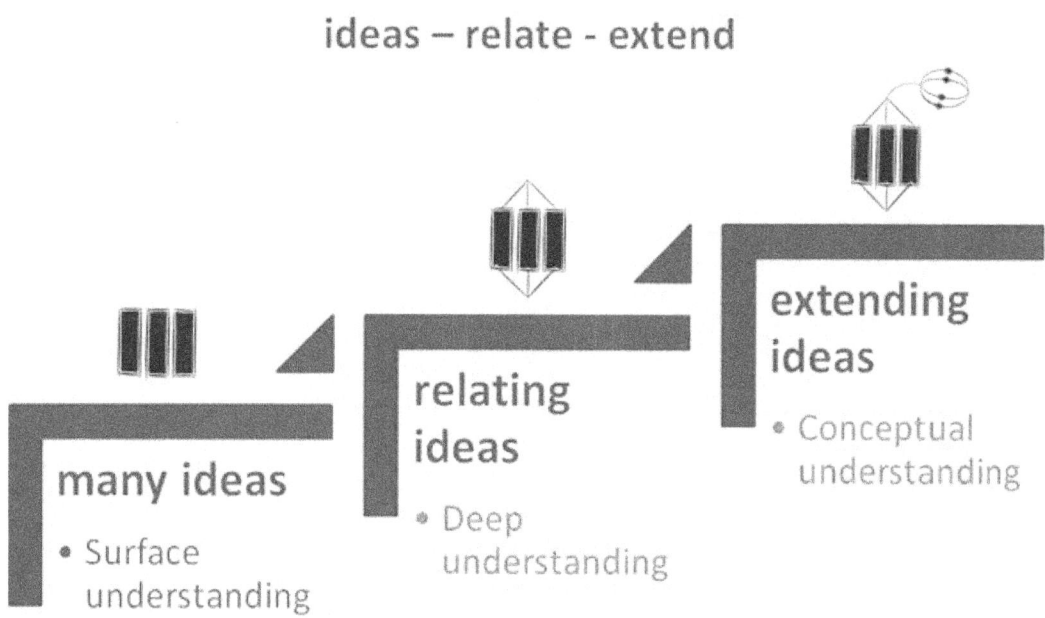

SOLO helps teachers and students differentiate learning tasks and learning outcomes for both **declarative and functioning knowledge outcomes**. For functioning knowledge, they can use it to differentiate surface, deep and conceptual levels of learning outcomes.

The self-assessment rubrics that follow show how SOLO Taxonomy can used to assess functioning knowledge (Exhibit 1.3) and declarative knowledge (Exhibit 1.4).

Exhibit 1.3: SOLO self-assessment rubric for functioning knowledge

Functioning knowledge	**Prestructural** *Needs help*	**Unistructural** *If directed*	**Multistructural** *Aware but no reasons, has a go, makes mistakes*	**Relational** *Purposeful, strategic, identifies mistakes*	**Extended abstract** *New ways, feedback, role model, teaches others*
Learning intention [verb] [content] [context]	I need help to start.	I can [xxxx] if directed or shown exactly what to do.	I can [xxxx] but I don't know why or when so it is trial and error. I make mistakes.	I can [xxxx], know why and when, am strategic or purposeful and find and correct my mistakes …	… **and** I seek feedback to improve, help others, am a role model and find new ways of doing [xxxx].

Note: Related online resources are the HookED SOLO Functioning Knowledge Rubric Generator (http://pamhook.com/solo-apps/functioning-knowledge-rubric-generator) and a comic strip example of this rubric (http://issuu.com/pamhook/docs/solo_functioningrubric).

Exhibit 1.4: SOLO self-assessment rubric for declarative knowledge

Declarative knowledge	**Prestructural** Needs help	**Unistructural** One relevant idea	**Multistructural** Several relevant ideas	**Relational** Linked ideas	**Extended abstract** Extended ideas
Learning intention [verb] [content] [context]	I need help to start.	My [learning outcome] has one relevant idea.	My [learning outcome] has several relevant ideas …	… **and** I can link these ideas …	… **and** I can look at them in a new way.

Note: Related online resources are the HookED SOLO Declarative Knowledge Rubric Generator (http://pamhook.com/solo-apps/declarative-knowledge-rubric-generator) and a comic strip example of this rubric (http://issuu.com/pamhook/docs/solo_declarativerubric).

What is social inquiry?

Social inquiry is a pedagogical approach that encourages students to think like social scientists when making meaning of social phenomena in local, national and global contexts.

Students doing social inquiry learn to collect and analyse data to identify causes, predict occurrences and develop evidence-based intervention programmes to address the phenomena in some way (as Exhibit 1 illustrated in the Introduction).

As described in the New Zealand Curriculum (Ministry of Education 2007, p 30), the process of learning to think like a social scientist involves learning to:

- ask questions, gather information and background ideas, and examine relevant current issues
- explore and analyse people's values and perspectives
- consider the ways in which people make decisions and participate in social action
- reflect on and evaluate the understandings they have developed and the responses that may be required.

These steps form part of the social inquiry process and are used to explore contemporary social phenomena. Many initial inquiries explore citizenship through local social phenomena with questions like:

- What matters most to young people in your local area? (SOLO multistructural task)
- How and why has young people's access to these opportunities and resources changed over time? (SOLO relational task)
- How can we best work with others to give young people continued access to these opportunities and resources in the future? (SOLO extended abstract task)

In other social studies contexts, students can study national and global phenomena such as:

- leadership
- government control
- transport
- human rights
- globalisation
- immigration
- aid programmes
- conflict
- financial and employment literacy.

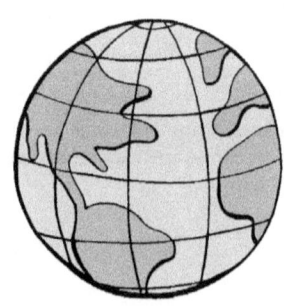

How do SOLO and social inquiry work together?

To successfully undertake social inquiry, students must develop:

- skilled and active **functioning knowledge outcomes**, such as:
  - research and communication skills to assess and manage data presented in many different modalities
  - critical thinking skills to explain, evaluate and reflect on many different kinds of evidence
  - persuasive argument skills in both oral and written language
- deep and conceptual **declarative knowledge outcomes** – for example, describing, explaining, evaluating and reflecting on social phenomena by writing, talking or drawing.

SOLO and social inquiry tasks

The steps in the social inquiry process align well with the levels in SOLO Taxonomy as they cover bringing in ideas (unistructural and multistructural), relating ideas (relational) and extending ideas by looking at them in new ways (extended abstract). The following are some examples.

"Finding out information", at the SOLO multistructural level, is suitable for early steps in the inquiry process. Students bring in ideas as they work to identify:

- background and historical knowledge
- current issues
- concepts and patterns
- sources of information.

"Exploring values and perspectives", at the SOLO relational level, follows on from bringing in relevant ideas and information. At this stage, students link ideas when they *explain causes* of people's values, viewpoints, perspectives and beliefs and *explain effects* of people's values, viewpoints, perspectives and beliefs on their responses and so on.

"Reflecting and evaluating", at the SOLO extended abstract level, requires deep understanding before students can conceptualise about the "big picture" ideas. At this stage, students extend their thinking in new ways as they reflect on:

- what else we need to know
- why the information was produced
- whose perspective was used.

Exhibit 1.5 illustrates in more detail how SOLO Taxonomy levels align with steps in the social inquiry process, based on a model from the New Zealand Ministry of Education.

SOLO and social inquiry outcomes

Because task and outcome can be at different levels of SOLO, students can achieve each step in the social inquiry process at a different level of success (cognitive complexity). The following selection of self-assessment rubrics and examples of students' work illustrate how this separation of task and outcome works for:

- identifying the focus of the learning, a relational or extended abstract task for which students can achieve an outcome at any SOLO level (Exhibit 1.6)
- reflecting and evaluating, an extended abstract task for which students can achieve an outcome at any SOLO level (Exhibit 1.7)
- finding out information, a multistructural task with potential for outcomes at any SOLO level (Exhibit 1.8), with a sample of work showing an extended abstract outcome (Exhibit 1.9)
- exploring values and perspectives, a relational task with potential for outcomes at any SOLO level (Exhibit 1.10), with a sample of work showing an extended abstract outcome (Exhibit 1.11).

Exhibit 1.5: SOLO Taxonomy levels apply throughout the social inquiry process

| Focus of learning | Concepts | Conceptual understandings |

Developed through ↓

| Finding out information | Exploring values and perspectives | Considering responses and decisions |
| *Bringing in ideas (multistructural)* | *Linking ideas (relational)* | *Extending ideas (extended abstract)* |

| Reflecting and evaluating | *Extending ideas (extended abstract)* |

Leading to ↓

- What do we know about this?
- What does this mean for us and others?

Extending ideas (extended abstract)

↓

- What further learning do we need?
- What might be done about it?

Extending ideas (extended abstract)

Source: Model for social inquiry process adapted from Ministry of Education (2008)

Exhibit 1.6: SOLO self-assessment rubric for identifying the focus of the learning (relational/extended abstract task)

Identify focus of learning	**Prestructural**	**Unistructural**	**Multistructural**	**Relational**	**Extended abstract**
Identify **questions** we could ask	I need help to identify questions we could ask.	I can identify questions we could ask if I am prompted or directed.	I can identify questions we could ask but I am not sure if they are relevant.	I can identify questions we could ask and explain why they are relevant …	… **and** I can seek and act on feedback to improve the questions.
Identify **assumptions** we hold	I need help to identify assumptions we hold.	I can identify assumptions we hold if I am prompted or directed.	I can identify assumptions we hold but I am not sure if they are relevant.	I can identify assumptions we hold and explain why they are relevant …	… **and** I can seek and act on feedback to improve our assumptions.
Effective strategies					

Exhibit 1.7: SOLO self-assessment rubric for reflecting and evaluating (extended abstract task)

Reflecting and evaluating	Prestructural	Unistructural	Multistructural	Relational	Extended abstract
Reflect on: what else we need to know; why the information was produced; whose perspective was used	I need help to reflect on [xxx].	My reflection identifies one relevant idea about [xxx].	My reflection identifies several relevant ideas about [xxx] …	… **and** I can explain why these ideas are relevant …	… **and** I can make a generalisation about [xxx].
Evaluate the learning process; reliability of sources	I need help to evaluate [xxx].	My evaluation makes a claim about [xxx] …	… **and** I can elaborate on the meaning of the claim …	… **and** I can explain why the claim is relevant and reliable …	… **and** I can justify the claim using evidence.
Effective strategies					

Exhibit 1.8: SOLO self-assessment rubric for finding out information (multistructural task)

Finding out information	Prestructural	Unistructural	Multistructural	Relational	Extended abstract
Identify: • background and historical knowledge • current issues • concepts and patterns • sources of information	I need help to identify relevant […].	I can identify relevant […] if I am prompted or directed.	I can identify […] but I am not sure if they are relevant.	I can identify […] **and** explain why they are relevant …	… **and** I can seek and act on feedback to improve the […].
Effective strategies					

11

Exhibit 1.9: Student work sample for gathering information and identifying sources (extended abstract outcome)

Human Rights issues in Asia   Name: _____

The aim of this mini research is to show evidence of two things. First **gathering information** and referencing it and second, stating **viewpoints** on an issue. (see the rubrics for clarification).

Task One: Gathering information:
Pick a topic—google "human rights issues" and "China or Asia" and pick a focus for this inquiry

Aim to do the following:
- Inquiry focus: Child Labour in Gold Mines in South China
- Gather information (use the space provided)
- Reference your sources: (use the space provided)
- Critique your findings—are they fact, common knowledge or opinion—how do you know the validity/reliability of them? What perspective is it from?

Topic: Child Labour in Gold Mines in South China

In South China, child labour in Gold Mines is a human rights issue. Nearly 1 million children work in unregulated small-scale gold mines around South China. This is a big problem in other parts of the world too, but mainly in South China. These children are having to work in pits more than 15 meters deep, where they dig ore. They mix the ore with toxic mercury which they are exposed to, so that they can retrieve gold. Many children working in these mines don't go to school, some do but they find it hard to keep up with the schoolwork. Much of the work that they do in gold mines is prohibited under International law for anyone under the age of 18.

In the tunnels & mineshafts the children risk death from explosions, rock falls, and tunnel collapse. They breathe air filled with dust, and sometimes toxic gases. In the gold mines there is no protective gear like hardhats, or any correct methods for digging tunnels or handling explosives. Although they know the ore is dangerous, most do not know about the proper handling of mercury.

Some children mine alongside their families or friends after school, or in holidays. Some drop out of school to work full time. In the worst cases, children are trafficked to mine sites where they are forced to work in absolutely horrendous slave-like conditions.

These facts are written from the perspective of Human Rights Watch, and various other reporters who are concerned about this human rights issue. I haven't been able to find out if there is any progress being made in the last few years to try and help stop this, or if there are still more children out there risking their lives in the gold mines of South China. It would be interesting to know if any action being taken or not with this issue.

Sources:
- (m.hrw.org/news/2012/end-child-labor-gold-mines)
- (www.ilo.org/ipec/areas/Miningandquarrying/Moreabout(Chinmining)/lang--en/index.htm)
- (www.globalmarch.org/content/children-engaged-unsafe-mining)

Note: Red descriptors are a guide	Insufficient evidence **PRE-STRUCTURAL**	Achieving Below Standard **UNISTRUCTURAL**	Achieving at Level **MULTISTRUCTURAL**	Achieving at Level **RELATIONAL**	Achieving Above the Level / Achieving Well Above the level **EXTENDED ABSTRACT**
Gather Information - Graphs - Tables - Blogs - Oral recordings - Documentaries - News articles - Books - Websites - statistics - interviews - social media #tags etc	I need help to do this	I can find relevant information if I'm told where to look	I can find relevant information from **multiple sources and perspectives** ...and can keep a record of where and when found my information	...and my information is **detailed** ...and can keep a record of where and when I found my information so the information can be accessed by others. ...and I can show (e.g. annotate and or make links) that this information is reliable	...and my information shows **insight** ...and I can evaluate my research process by including ... - eg strengths and weaknesses - holes in my research - next steps/what I still need to find out

12

Exhibit 1.10: SOLO self-assessment rubric for exploring values and perspectives (relational task)

Exploring values and perspectives	Prestructural	Unistructural	Multistructural	Relational	Extended abstract
Exploring values and perspectives	I need help to explore values and perspectives.	I can explore values and perspectives if I am prompted or directed.	I can explore values and perspectives but I am not sure if they are relevant.	I can explore values and perspectives and explain why they are relevant …	… and I can seek and act on feedback to improve my exploration.
Explain causes of people's values, perspectives and beliefs	I can identify people's values, perspectives and beliefs but I need help to explain causes.	My explanation identifies one relevant cause.	My explanation identifies several relevant causes …	… and I can explain why these causes are relevant …	… and I can make a generalisation about the causes.
Explain effects of people's values, perspectives and beliefs on their responses	I can identify people's values, perspectives and beliefs but I need help to explain their effects on people's responses	My explanation identifies one relevant effect.	My explanation identifies several relevant effects …	…and I can explain why these effects are relevant …	… and I can make a generalisation about the effects.
Compare and contrast people's values and/or perspectives	I can identify people's values and/or perspectives but I need help to compare and contrast them.	My comparison identifies one relevant similarity and/or difference.	My comparison identifies several relevant similarities and differences …	… and I can explain why these similarities and differences are relevant …	… and I can make a generalisation about the similarities and differences.
Classify values and perspectives as "stated" or "missing"	I can identify people's values and/or perspectives but I need help to classify them.	My classification identifies one relevant group.	My classification identifies both relevant groups …	… and I can explain why these groupings are relevant …	… and I can make a generalisation about the groups.
Effective strategies					

Exhibit 1.11: Student work sample for explaining viewpoints (extended abstract outcome)

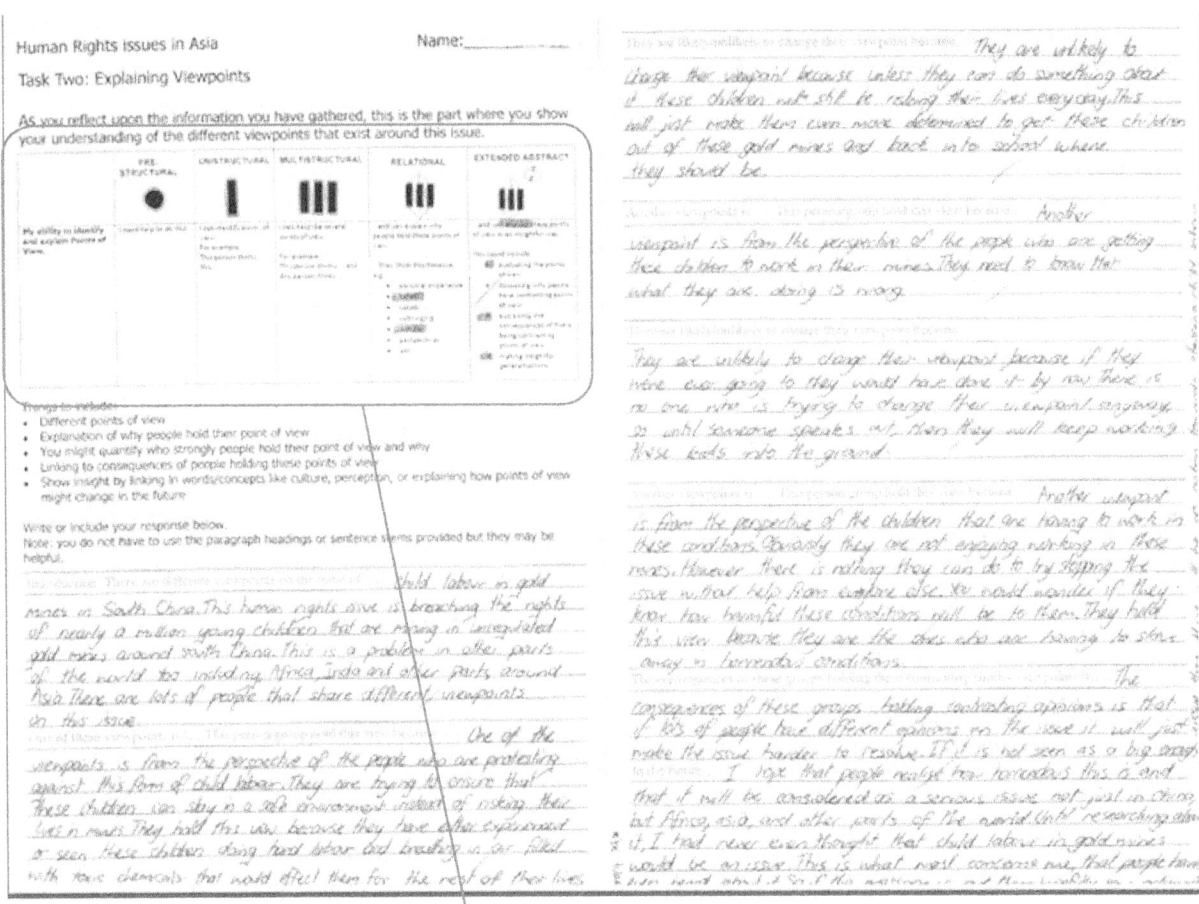

Note: This student has used highlighting to help them plan out and clarify their strategies for success – showing how rubrics can be useful for developing student agency.

2. Teaching approaches that enhance outcomes

SOLO is useful because you just know what you have to do. You just look at the SOLO map and start to answer the questions and you are away. Year 9 student, Lincoln High School

SOLO provides a robust, easily recognisable learning model backed by sound evidence. It informs a powerful pedagogical approach (constructive alignment) and can be used to enhance all aspects of effective teaching and learning (planning, monitoring and assessment) (Hook 2015).

In our experience, SOLO helps teachers adopt the four specific teaching approaches that Aitken and Sinnema (2008) identify in their Best Evidence Synthesis as enhancing outcomes for diverse learners in the social sciences – namely alignment, connection, community and interest.

This section provides examples of alignment, connection and community using New Zealand Curriculum concepts related to identity, culture and organisation; place and environment; continuity and change; and the economic world. Interest, the fourth desirable teaching approach, comes from choosing such contexts, which enable students to develop "democratic imagination, motivation and involvement" (Hayward 2012).

Alignment and SOLO

The Best Evidence Synthesis research finds that, in the social sciences, effective teachers align their teaching activities and teaching resources to the desired learning outcomes (Aitken and Sinnema 2008). They do this in several ways, including by:

- identifying prior knowledge
- aligning activities
- aligning resources to intended learning outcomes.

When teachers use SOLO, they make all of these teaching strategies easier as they can use the SOLO levels to describe the cognitive complexity of the task, the resource or effective strategy and/or the student learning outcome. In the discussion that follows, we explore how using each of these strategies in combination with SOLO enhances student outcomes.

Determine prior knowledge

SOLO levels can be used to assess prior knowledge for:

- **functioning knowledge** (knowing how to) outcomes – for example, an assessment may show that students have a SOLO unistructural level of performance outcome. That is, they are able to model a performance outcome if directed or by copying a coach but are unable to successfully complete the task independently (see Exhibit 1.3 in Section 1)
- **declarative knowledge** (knowing about) – for example, an assessment may show that students have a surface or SOLO multistructural level of understanding before they start. That is, they have many loose ideas but cannot relate these ideas to show deeper understanding of the big ideas or integrating principles (see Exhibit 1.4 in Section 1).

This assessment can be communicated verbally, or by using symbols, hexagons and/or hand signs (Exhibit 2.1).

Using SOLO hexagons. SOLO hexagons (based on an idea from Hodgson 1992) offer a strategy for enhancing higher order thinking and systems thinking in individual work and small-group discussions. Teachers use SOLO hexagons to determine prior knowledge, scaffold student writing and oral language, conduct formative assessment, and revise and/or extend student thinking (Hook 2015, p 36). The following examples show how SOLO hexagons can be used to determine the extent and depth of prior knowledge. They are also effective in formative or summative assessment.

The general approach to a SOLO hexagon activity, in which students may work on their own or as a class, is as follows:

1. Students identify and describe content (using symbols, ideas, text and images) on individual hexagons.
2. Students make links between the hexagons, annotating any links with reasons.
3. Students extend their thinking by making a generalisation about the big idea in any cluster or clusters of hexagons.

Exhibit 2.1: Student pointing to the level of learning outcome on a SOLO self-assessment visual rubric

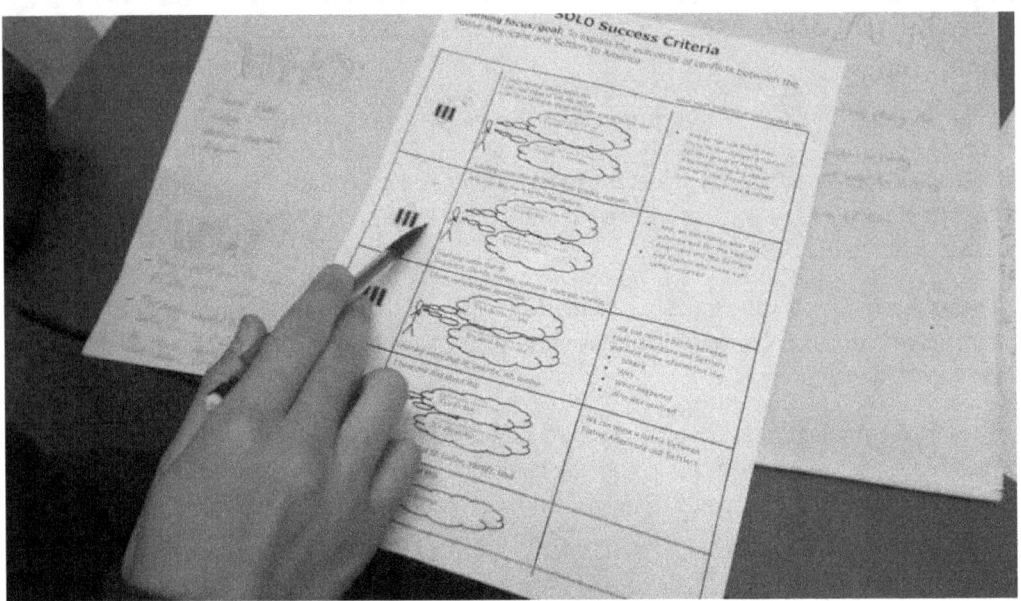

Exhibit 2.2 outlines this approach as well as setting out some examples of linked ideas and extended thinking about Russia that students have made through this process. The final tessellations are a great prompt for students to undertake analysis and big picture thinking.

With a simple rubric, students can then reflect on the SOLO level of the outcome from the activity:

- prestructural outcome – the learner has no relevant ideas on the hexagons
- unistructural outcome – the learner has one relevant idea on a hexagon; surface thinking
- multistructural outcome – the learner has many relevant ideas on the hexagons; surface thinking
- relational outcome – the learner has linked or related ideas on the hexagons; deep thinking
- extended abstract outcome – the learner has extended ideas about the clusters of hexagons; big-picture conceptual thinking.

Students can also add to the outcomes from this activity over time as their content vocabulary and understanding grow.

Using SOLO learning logs. By using a SOLO-coded learning log (or entry and exit tickets to and from a unit of learning), teachers and students can clearly identify what progress students have made over time as well as appropriate next steps (Hook 2015, p 29). Template 2.1 shows a learning log along with a self-assessment rubric for reflecting on levels of knowing. Exhibit 2.3 sets out an example of how a student has assessed their level of knowing before and after a task on explaining Japanese youth culture and has reflected on their learning in their learning log.

Constructive alignment of learning intentions and learning activities

Constructive alignment is a principle of seeking alignment between:

- what needs to be learnt (curriculum goals)
- what the students will do (learning intentions)
- the learning activities provided
- how the learning outcomes from these activities will be assessed or demonstrated (Biggs 1999; Biggs and Tang 2007).

In our experience of working with teachers, SOLO is key to this process of aligning learning activities to desired outcomes (curriculum goals or achievement objectives) (Hook 2015, p 21).

Exhibit 2.4 shows the alignment of the master goal or achievement objective with differentiated learning intentions, success criteria and learning tasks.

Exhibit 2.2: Using SOLO hexagons to determine prior knowledge

Learning goals	Success criteria
To define and describe aspects of Russia	I will know this when I can: • bring in ideas (multistructural) • make links between ideas (relational) • explain more complex links to show insight (extended abstract).

Step 1: Bringing in new ideas

1. Think–pair–share: As you think about what you know of Russia, list as many words or ideas as you can that might be relevant to understanding Russia.
2. One person cuts out the hexagons; the other writes the class's ideas from the board on to the hexagons.

This is **multistructural** thinking.

Appreciate the moment. "Well done, look at all the ideas we now have to work with."

Example

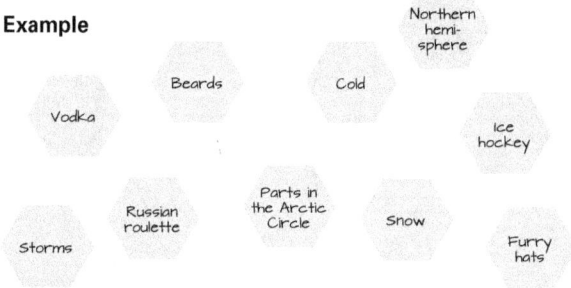

Step 2: Making links

Move your ideas around and see what links you can make between them. This is **relational** thinking.

Examples

Because it's near the Arctic Circle, it is cold so they wear furry hats and have beards and play ice hockey.

Russia is in the northern hemisphere and parts of it are in the Arctic Circle so it's cold and they have storms.

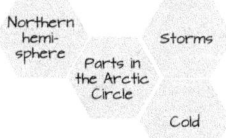

Step 3: Complex links or insight

As you consider the links you have made, where you have linked more than two ideas, what is the overall thing they have in common?

This is **extended abstract** thinking: concluding, generalising, justifying, synthesising.

Examples

The physical location of a country can influence the development of its unique culture.

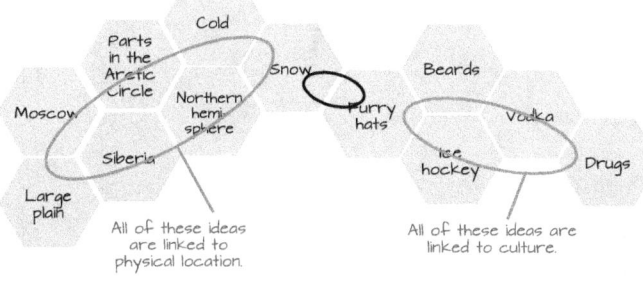

The actual location of Russia in the world is responsible for the climate and conditions in Russia.

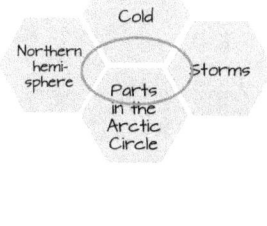

Template 2.1: SOLO learning log and self-assessment rubric to determine prior knowledge and next steps

Generic rubric for thinking about levels of knowing

Thought bubbles	Rubric descriptor
What you do knowledge (functional knowledge): *I could teach someone else how to ...* Showing what you know (declarative knowledge): *Overall ... because ... because ...*	... **and** I can link my ideas to the big picture or look at these ideas in a new or different way. Learning verbs that fit: *generalise, predict, evaluate*
What you do knowledge (functional knowledge): *You do this ... because ...* Showing what you know (declarative knowledge): *It's about this ... because ...*	I have several ideas about this and I can make links between them ... Learning verbs that fit: *sequence, classify, explain, compare, contrast, analyse*
What you do knowledge (functional knowledge): *You do this ... and ...* Showing what you know (declarative knowledge): *It's about this ... and ...*	I have several ideas about this. Learning verbs that fit: *describe, list, outline*
What you do knowledge (functional knowledge): *You do this ...* Showing what you know (declarative knowledge): *It's about this ...*	I have one idea about this. Learning verbs that fit: *define, identify, label*
Ummm ...	I am not sure about this.

SOLO learning progress

The learning intention, goal or topic:

What I already know is:

Some things I know that I do not yet know are:

My starting level of knowing is: *(Check the rubric opposite and circle the symbol that best represents your starting level.)*

Reflection

What I now know is:

Some things I know that I do not yet know are:

My current level of knowing is: *(Check the rubric opposite and circle the symbol that best represents your current level.)*

My next steps for improvement are:

© Pam Hook, HookED, and Craig Perry 2016. All rights reserved.

Exhibit 2.3: Student's reflection on level of knowing before and after a task on explaining Japanese youth culture

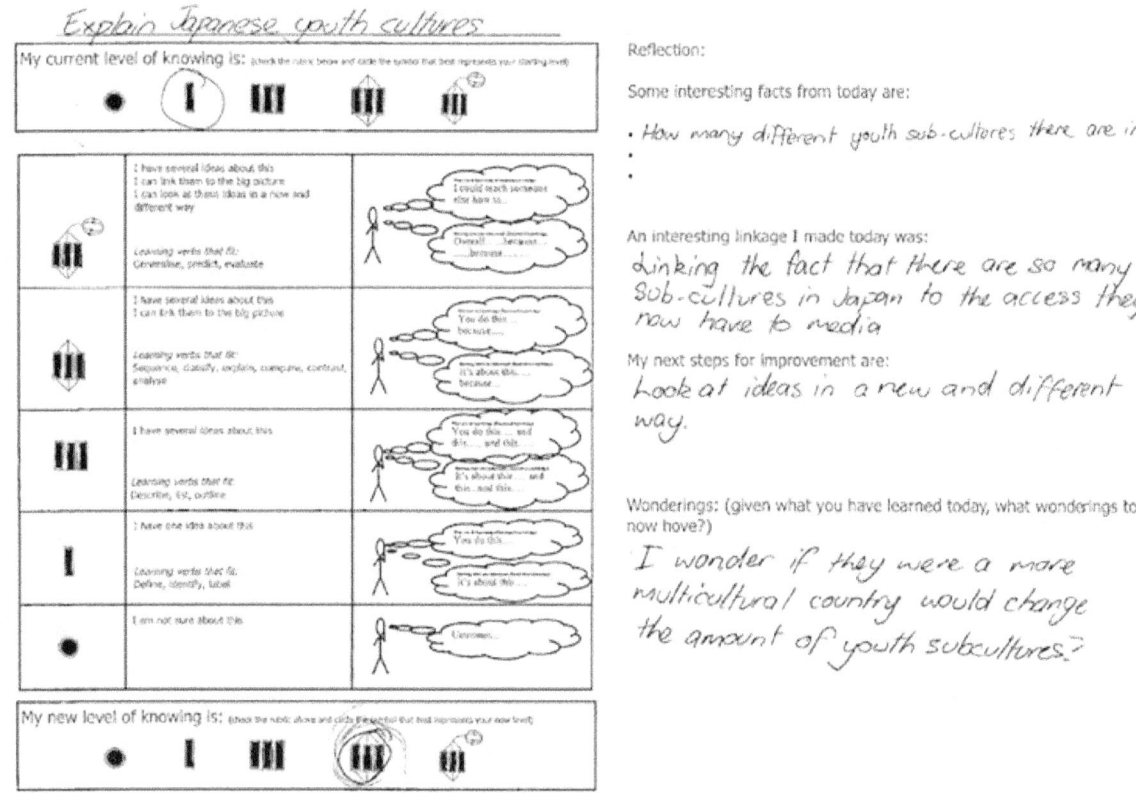

Exhibit 2.4: Constructive alignment in overview

	Curriculum goal or achievement objective	**Learning intentions** [verb] [content] [context]	**Success criteria**	**Learning activities or experiences**
Key question	What do the students need to understand or demonstrate?	What must the students do to reach the goal?	How will students know if they have achieved the goal?	What activities will help students in completing the tasks and ultimately reaching the curriculum goal?
Key teaching strategies	Align learning intentions, success criteria and learning activities with the mastery goal to help students to achieve it.	Develop learning intentions to help students achieve the mastery goal. Use SOLO to differentiate each learning intention based on the command verbs used (Exhibit 2.5).	Develop differentiated success criteria for each learning intention. Use SOLO to differentiate the success criteria for each learning intention.	Align the nature of the learning activity with the SOLO level of the learning intention and, in turn, with the mastery goal.

Exhibit 2.5 shows how command verbs at different levels of SOLO can be used to differentiate the learning activities at different levels of cognitive complexity. To differentiate a learning intention, teachers code it against SOLO based on the levels of cognitive complexity of its command verb. The structure of a learning intention is therefore:

LI: [verb][content] [context] – SOLO level of task

As noted in Section 1, with SOLO the cognitive complexity of the task and outcome can be at different levels. Students can therefore achieve a multistructural task (eg, *describe*) at any of the SOLO levels. With this separation of task and outcome, it is also possible to differentiate success criteria for each learning intention against SOLO Taxonomy.

Exhibit 2.5: SOLO declarative knowledge verbs aligned to differentiated learning activities

SOLO level	Purpose of learning activities	Command verbs
Unistructural	Bring in an idea	*define, identify, label, match*
Multistructural	Bring in ideas	*describe, list, outline*
Relational	Link or connect ideas	*sequence, classify, explain causes, explain effects, compare, contrast, analyse*
Extended abstract	Extend ideas some place new	*generalise, predict, evaluate*

Outlined below are several useful SOLO-linked strategies for achieving constructive alignment.

Using the SOLO "plus 1" strategy. When using SOLO levels to describe students' prior knowledge, teachers can make use of the SOLO "plus 1" strategy to plan appropriately challenging next steps for learning (Hook 2015, p 22). In this approach, teachers design their teaching activities at one level above the level of cognitive challenge indicated for students' prior knowledge.

Using the example of a learning activity focused on the impact of the Gallipoli campaign on New Zealand's national identity, Exhibit 2.6 demonstrates how SOLO "plus 1" can be used to good effect in planning next steps.

Using a SOLO-differentiated task sheet and SOLO verbs. Teachers also use SOLO verbs to create task sheets to develop and challenge students' thinking (Hook 2015, p 25). Such tasks could be used as SOLO stations activities, where each station offers a range of activities at a particular SOLO level.

Exhibit 2.7 presents an example of a SOLO-differentiated task sheet. The self-assessment rubric that follows (Exhibit 2.8) can be used to evaluate the outcomes from that task sheet.

Using an NCEA-differentiated assessment. In New Zealand's National Certificate of Educational Achievement (NCEA), the achievement criteria for geographical understanding discriminate outcomes across three levels as follows:

- Achievement – demonstrate understanding
- Merit – demonstrate in-depth understanding
- Excellence – demonstrate comprehensive understanding.

The descriptors and their elaborations can be directly aligned with SOLO multistructural, relational and extended abstract outcomes as set out in the HookED SOLO Explain causes self-assessment rubric (Hook 2015, p 55). Exhibit 2.9 details this relationship.

Using a SOLO Learning Intention Generator and SOLO verbs. The HookED SOLO Learning Intention Generator (http://pamhook.com/solo-apps/learning-intention-generator) helps teachers and students use SOLO verbs to create a series of tasks of increasing cognitive complexity (Hook 2015, p 21). Exhibit 2.10 presents an example of the kinds of tasks that might result from this approach for a teacher planning a scheme of work on leadership.

Exhibit 2.6: Using SOLO "plus 1" to relate the level of prior knowledge to an appropriate next step

SOLO level	Prior knowledge	Next steps *SOLO "plus 1" strategy*
Prestructural	I need help to understand the claim that the Gallipoli campaign helped foster a sense of national identity.	**Describe** New Zealand (place and people who lived there) before the campaign. **Describe** the campaign **Describe the causes** of the campaign **Describe the effects** of the campaign on the places and the people involved.
Unistructural	I can give one reason in support of the claim.	**Describe** New Zealand society after the campaign **Compare and contrast** New Zealand society before and after the campaign **Explain the effects** of the campaign on the places and people involved (short, medium and long term)
Multistructural	I can give several reasons in support of the claim …	**Explain how and why** New Zealand society was changed by the campaign.
Relational	… **and** I can explain why these reasons support the claim …	**Explain** why ANZAC Day was so important to New Zealanders in the past and continues to be so today. **Describe** other significant events that changed New Zealanders' sense of themselves and their place in the world.
Extended abstract	… **and** I can evaluate the strength of the claim.	

Exhibit 2.7: SOLO-differentiated task sheet

Write three paragraphs that answer the following questions:

1. **Describe** the [social issue, idea, theme]. *(Finding out information)*
2. **Explain** how the [social issue, idea, theme] affected people's lives and the values and perspectives they held. *(Exploring values and perspectives)*
3. **Evaluate** people's responses to the decisions made in the [social issue, idea, theme]. *(Considering responses and decisions)*

Exhibit 2.8: SOLO self-assessment rubric for outcomes from the SOLO-differentiated task sheet (Exhibit 2.7)

SOLO level	Describe task	Explain task	Evaluate task
Prestructural	I need help to describe [social issue, idea, theme].	I need help to explain how [social issue, idea, theme] affected people's lives and their values and perspectives.	I need help to evaluate the people's responses to the decisions made in [social issue, idea, theme].
Unistructural	My description identifies one relevant aspect of [social issue, idea, theme].	My explanation identifies one relevant effect of [social issue, idea, theme] on people's lives and their values and perspectives.	My evaluation makes one relevant claim about the people's responses to the decisions made in [social issue, idea, theme] and one relevant claim about an alternative response or decision.
Multistructural	My description identifies several relevant aspects of [social issue, idea, theme] …	My explanation identifies several relevant effects of [social issue, idea, theme] on people's lives and their values and perspectives …	My evaluation makes several relevant claims about the people's responses to the decisions made in [social issue, idea, theme] **and** several relevant claims about alternative responses or decisions …
Relational	… **and** explains how these aspects affected the lives of the [insert social identifier] people …	… **and** provides reasons and examples to explain these effects …	… **and** provides reasons and examples in support of each claim …
Extended abstract	… **and** suggest alternative actions that [eg, the government] could have taken.	… **and** looks at this in a new way by imagining the effects that alternative actions may have had on people's lives and their values and perspectives.	… **and** provides reasons and examples in support of each claim. It makes a judgement about the actual and possible decisions and responses.

Exhibit 2.9: SOLO levels and NCEA achievement criteria applied to learning outcomes for "Explain a large natural environment"

Achievement	Achievement with merit	Achievement with excellence
Demonstrate geographic understanding of a large natural environment.	Demonstrate in-depth geographic understanding of a large natural environment.	Demonstrate comprehensive geographic understanding of a large natural environment.
This involves: • explaining aspects of the large natural environment • including supporting case study evidence.	This involves • explaining, in detail, aspects of the large natural environment • including detailed supporting case study evidence.	This involves • fully explaining aspects of the large natural environment including the use of geographic terminology and concepts, showing insight • integrating comprehensive supporting case study evidence.
SOLO Explain causes rubric – multistructural	SOLO Explain causes rubric – relational	SOLO Explain causes rubric – extended abstract

Exhibit 2.10: Using the HookED SOLO Learning Intention Generator and SOLO verbs to create tasks of increasing cognitive complexity

Level 4 Social Sciences — **Social Studies**

Achievement objective: Understand how the ways in which leadership is acquired and exercised have consequences for communities and societies.

Visual map of the achievement objective

- Ways in which leadership is acquired (*How was leadership acquired?*) — Method 1, Method 2, Method 3
- Ways in which leadership is exercised (*How was leadership exercised?*) — Method 1, Method 2, Method 3
- Consequences for communities and societies:
  - short term — positive, negative, unaffected
  - medium term — positive, negative, unaffected
  - long term — positive, negative, unaffected

Learning intentions to …

Bring in ideas	Link/relate ideas	Extend ideas
Define leadership. **List** ways in which leadership is acquired eg, democracy, islamocracy, monarchy, oligarchy. **Describe** one or more methods of acquiring leadership **List** ways in which leadership is exercised eg, authoritarian, democratic, free rein, narcissistic. **Describe** one or more methods of exercising leadership.	**Classify** methods for acquiring/exercising leadership. **Compare and contrast** methods for acquiring/exercising leadership. **Explain the consequences** of acquiring/exercising leadership using Method 1 for communities and societies. *[positive, negative, unaffected] [short, medium, long term]*	**Make a generalisation** about the method of acquiring/exercising leadership and the consequences for communities and societies. *[short, medium, long term]* **Evaluate the extent to which** the method of acquiring/exercising leadership has consequences for communities and societies. *[short, medium, long term]*

Note: To access the HookED SOLO Learning Intention Generator, go to: http://pamhook.com/solo-apps/learning-intention-generator

Aligning resources and/or effective strategies

Resources and effective strategies can be coded against different levels of SOLO in a similar approach to coding learning activities (Hook 2015, p 16).

Using e-learning resources. Teachers can use SOLO to help them choose the most effective strategies (e-learning tools or thinking skills) to support student learning outcomes. By aligning learning supports (thinking strategies and e-learning tools) with learning experiences based on SOLO levels, they can add choice and challenge to learning (Exhibit 2.11). Even when strategies can be used across all levels of SOLO outcome – for bringing in ideas, linking ideas or extending ideas – identifying how the e-learning tool is being used in this instance brings purpose to students' efforts.

Exhibit 2.11: Examples of thinking strategies and e-learning differentiated against SOLO levels

Unistructural	Multistructural	Relational	Extended abstract
Strategies for bringing in ideas		**Strategies for connecting ideas**	**Strategies for extending ideas**
HOT SOLO Define map and self-assessment rubric	HookED SOLO hexagons	HookED SOLO hexagons	HookED SOLO hexagons
de Bono Red Hat thinking	HOT SOLO Describe map and self-assessment rubric	HOT SOLO Sequence, Classify, Compare and contrast, and Analyse maps and self-assessment rubrics	HOT SOLO Generalise, Predict and Evaluate maps and self-assessment rubrics
Google "Define" strategy (type "Define" in front of a word in Google search to access its definition)	de Bono White Hat thinking		HookED SOLO Describe ++ map and self-assessment rubric
	Brainstorming	HookED SOLO Explain causes, Explain effects, and Analogy maps and self-assessment rubrics	de Bono Blue Hat and Green Hat thinking
	Instagrok: www.instagrok.com		"What if" questions
	Google Maps: www.google.co.nz/maps	de Bono Yellow Hat and Black Hat thinking	Rationale: http://rationale.austhink.com
	Earthviewer: www.hhmi.org/biointeractive/earthviewer	de Bono CoRT Plus Minus Interesting routine	Values Exchange all schools project: www.vxcommunity.com
	National Geographic World Atlas (iPad) https://itunes.apple.com/gb/app/national-geographic-world/id364733950	Explain Everything app: www.morriscooke.com/?p=134	Minecraft: https://minecraft.net
		GapMinder: www.gapminder.org	

Students can create a toolbox of thinking and e-learning strategies categorised by how the strategies help them bring in ideas, connect ideas or extend ideas – outcomes at the different levels of SOLO. For example, a student will sort strategies according to SOLO levels and explain the sorting by stating "these strategies are at a multistructural level because they help me bring in ideas while these are at a relational level because they help me connect or link ideas".

Using SOLO visual maps and self-assessment rubrics. The HOT and HookED SOLO visual maps and self-assessment rubrics are effective strategies students can use to learn the process steps of each verb – *describe*, *compare* etc – and they can use the maps in particular to draft their written language outcomes (Hook 2015, p 39) (Exhibit 2.12). The maps prompt for surface, deep and conceptual understanding and help students structure their writing in simple sentences, complex sentences and paragraphs.

For detailed instructions on how to use the SOLO maps, see Hook and Mills (2011). You can also find animations for many of the SOLO maps on YouTube (**http://tinyurl.com/hnpd643**).

Exhibit 2.12: Overview of HOT and HookED maps linked to SOLO Taxonomy

Prestructural	Unistructural	Multistructural	Relational	Extended abstract
	Define	Describe	Sequence	Generalise
			Classify	Predict
			Compare and contrast	Evaluate
			Explain cause and effect	Describe ++
			Analyse part–whole	
			Explain causes	
			Explain effects	
			Form an analogy	

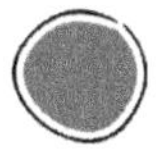

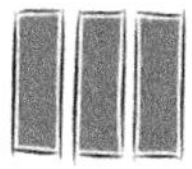

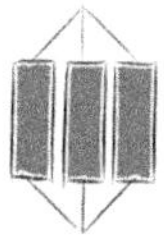

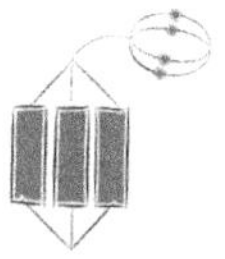

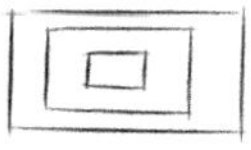

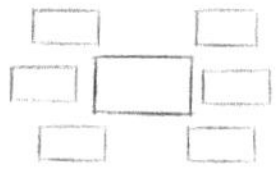

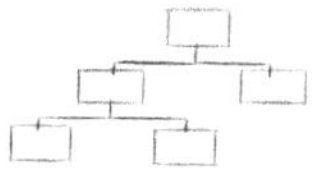

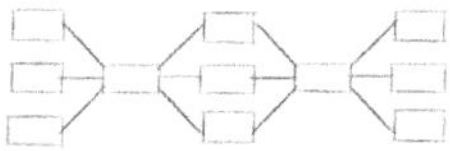

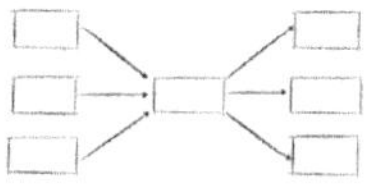

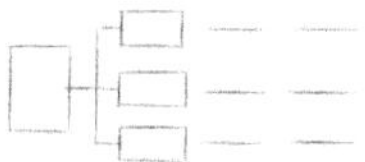

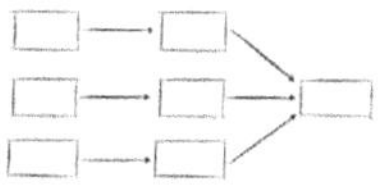

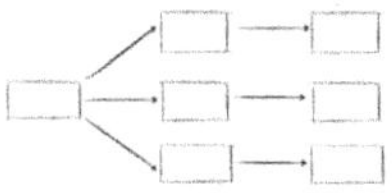

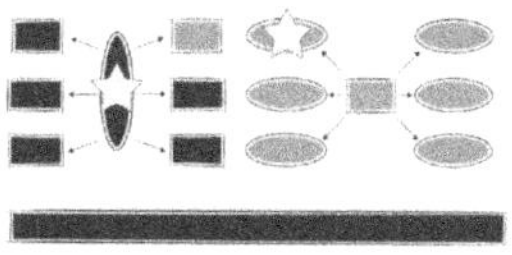

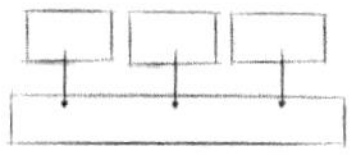

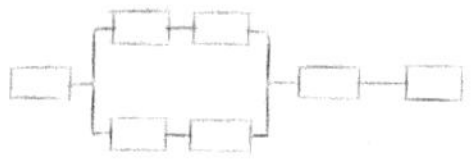

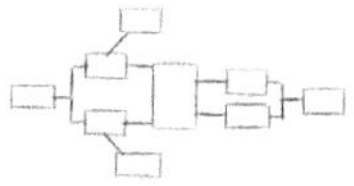

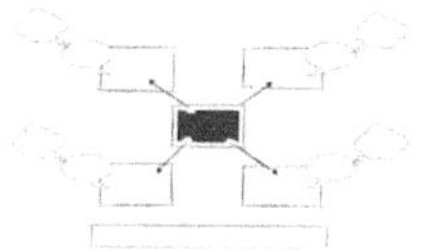

Differentiated success criteria (self-assessment rubrics) are introduced when students write from their draft thinking on the maps.

Given the simplicity of the SOLO levels, students can co-construct the rubrics with teachers and, after some practice, make their own self-assessment rubrics (see Hook and Mills 2011 for examples).

Highlighting text with SOLO levels. When examples of student work at different levels are shared as exemplars, students highlight the sections of the text or connectives that show loose ideas, connected ideas or extended ideas (Hook and Cassé 2013, p 12). Highlighting is also a useful strategy in activities where students take the text at one SOLO level and modify it so that it shows the structure of the level above or the level below.

Exhibit 2.13 illustrates this process through the example of writing a generalisation, which comprises: a HOT SOLO Generalise self-assessment rubric and vocabulary to scaffold the response (2.13(a)); an exemplar in which students have highlighted the higher-order thinking connectives (2.13(b)); and instructions for students to self-assess their generalisations, with reference to the exemplar and self-assessment rubric (2.13(c)).

Exhibit 2.13: Writing a generalisation about "Why people use the Stockton Plateau for mining"

(a) Self-assessment rubric and vocabulary prompts

Writing a generalisation about:
Why people use the Stockton Plateau for mining

People use the Stockton Plateau for mining because …

Words and ideas you might use:

- Bituminous coal
- Geological reasons
- Economic reasons
- 20 yr life
- Location
- Workforce
- Accessibility
- Because (relational)
- Overall (extended abstract)

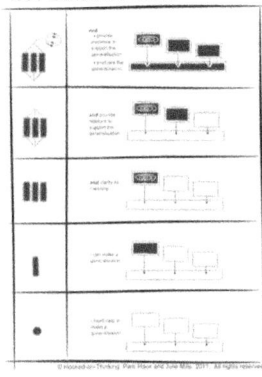

HOT Generalise Rubric

(b) Exemplar on which students highlight connectives for higher-order thinking

Writing a generalisation about:
Why people use the Stockton Plateau for mining

People use the Stockton Plateau for mining because over 70 million years ago there were conditions that were right for the formation of coal. There was a large area of swampy vegetation that was buried, had pressure and heat added and was given time to change from peat to high-grade bituminous coal. This area was then uplifted to form the Stockton Plateau. These are the geological reasons.

Other reasons are that the economic return from mining this area exceeds the investment required to access the coal. For example, in 2009 Solid Energy spent $200,000 in upgraded equipment. It must expect to recoup this investment over the 20 yr life of the mine. Because the mine is close to Westport, this location also has a workforce of accessible people. The mine employs about 650 people. The mine is also accessible via a rail link to Christchurch where the coal is exported to overseas markets.

Overall, these factors contribute to why this area is used for mining. The most significant being that the coal is there and it is economic to mine it.

Multistructural thinking   Relational thinking   Extended abstract thinking

continued …

Exhibit 2.13: Writing a generalisation about "Why people use the Stockton Plateau for mining" (continued)

(c) Instructions for students self-assessing their generalisations

> # Writing a generalisation about:
> ## Why people use the Stockton Plateau for mining
>
> Having read the exemplar, compare it with your own, grade your paragraphs against SOLO and decide what you should do next.
>
> My paragraphs are _____
>
> I think it sits here because ...
>
> My next step is to ...

Connection and SOLO

To develop students' ability to make connections, teachers need to help them to "use their own experiences **as a point of comparison** when learning about other people's experiences in different times, places and cultures" (Aitken and Sinnema 2008). Students need support to compare like a social scientist.

Making a comparison using one's own experiences as a reference point is an activity at the SOLO relational level. Below we look at three SOLO-based strategies that help students think in skilled and active ways when comparing the experiences of two groups, including making connections between their own experiences and those of others: HOT SOLO maps and self-assessment rubrics; SOLO hexagons; and SOLO reverse hexagons.

Connections through sequencing SOLO activities

The following two-hour lesson uses a sequence of SOLO strategies – SOLO hexagons, and HOT SOLO Compare and contrast and Generalise maps – to help students think deeply about the effect of European settlers on indigenous people (Exhibit 2.14). In this sequence, students:

- identified the content ideas on the hexagons and looked for reasons to make connections between ideas (2.14(a))
- used this thinking to explore connections of similarity and difference between treatments of indigenous people by European settlers in different locations and times using a HOT SOLO Compare and contrast map to draft ideas (2.14(b))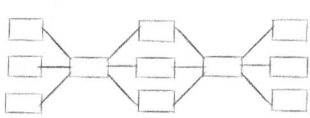
- wrote a generalisation integrating their new thinking about the effect of European settlers on indigenous people in different places and different times (2.14(c))
- self-assessed their generalisation based on the HOT SOLO Generalise self-assessment rubric (2.14(d)).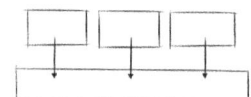

Templates 2.2 and 2.3 provide the HOT SOLO Compare and contrast map and self-assessment rubric.

Exhibit 2.14: Using SOLO strategies to think deeply about the effect of European settlers on indigenous people

(a) Using SOLO hexagons to explore connections among ideas

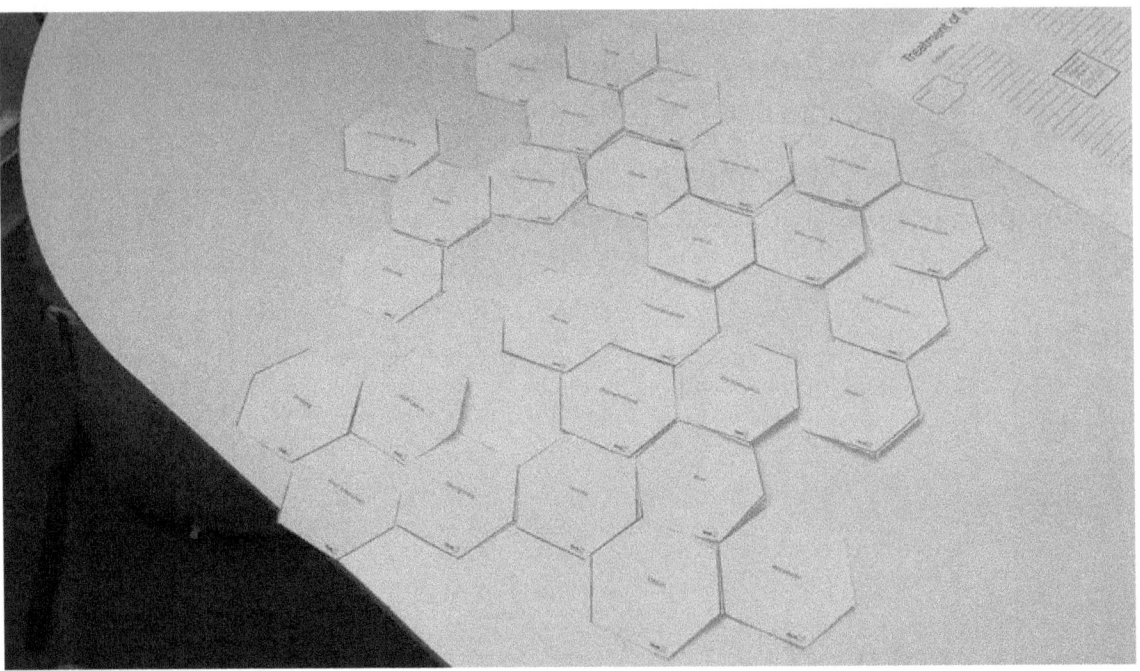

(b) Using a HOT SOLO Compare and contrast map to scaffold thinking

continued ...

Exhibit 2.14: Using SOLO strategies to think deeply about the effect of European settlers on indigenous people (continued)

(c) Writing a generalisation integrating new thinking recorded on the HOT SOLO Compare and contrast map

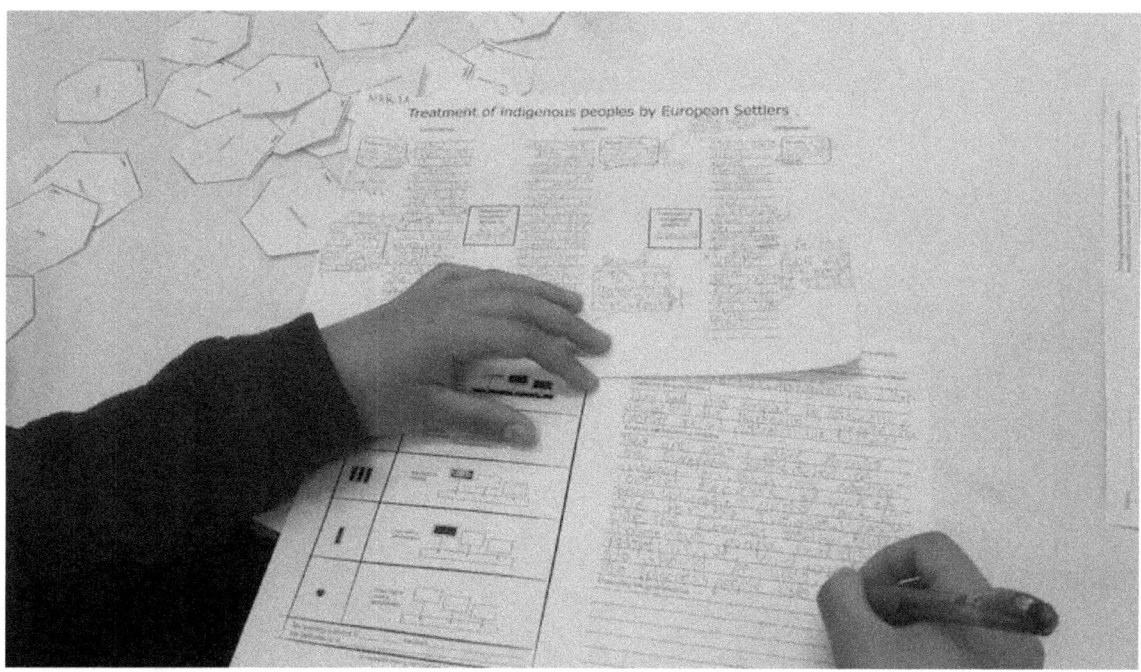

(d) Self-assessing the generalisation against the SOLO Generalise self-assessment rubric

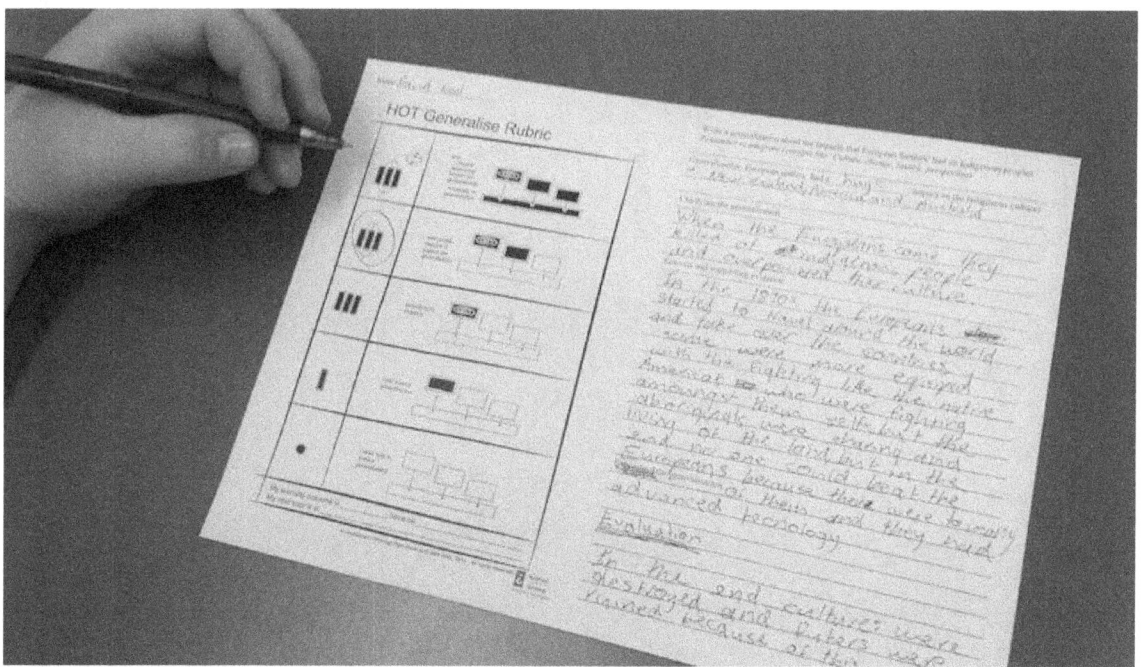

Connections through reverse SOLO hexagons

Another method of helping students make connections is to use SOLO hexagons and an adaptation called SOLO reverse hexagons (Template 2.4). In SOLO reverse hexagons, the teacher or students create the hexagon cluster and students are then challenged to create the images that explain the connections or explain the images that go with the connections.

Exhibit 2.15 gives an example of a student outcome on the topic of "factors affecting the health and wellbeing of a country" using HookED SOLO reverse hexagons.

Template 2.2: HOT SOLO Compare and contrast map

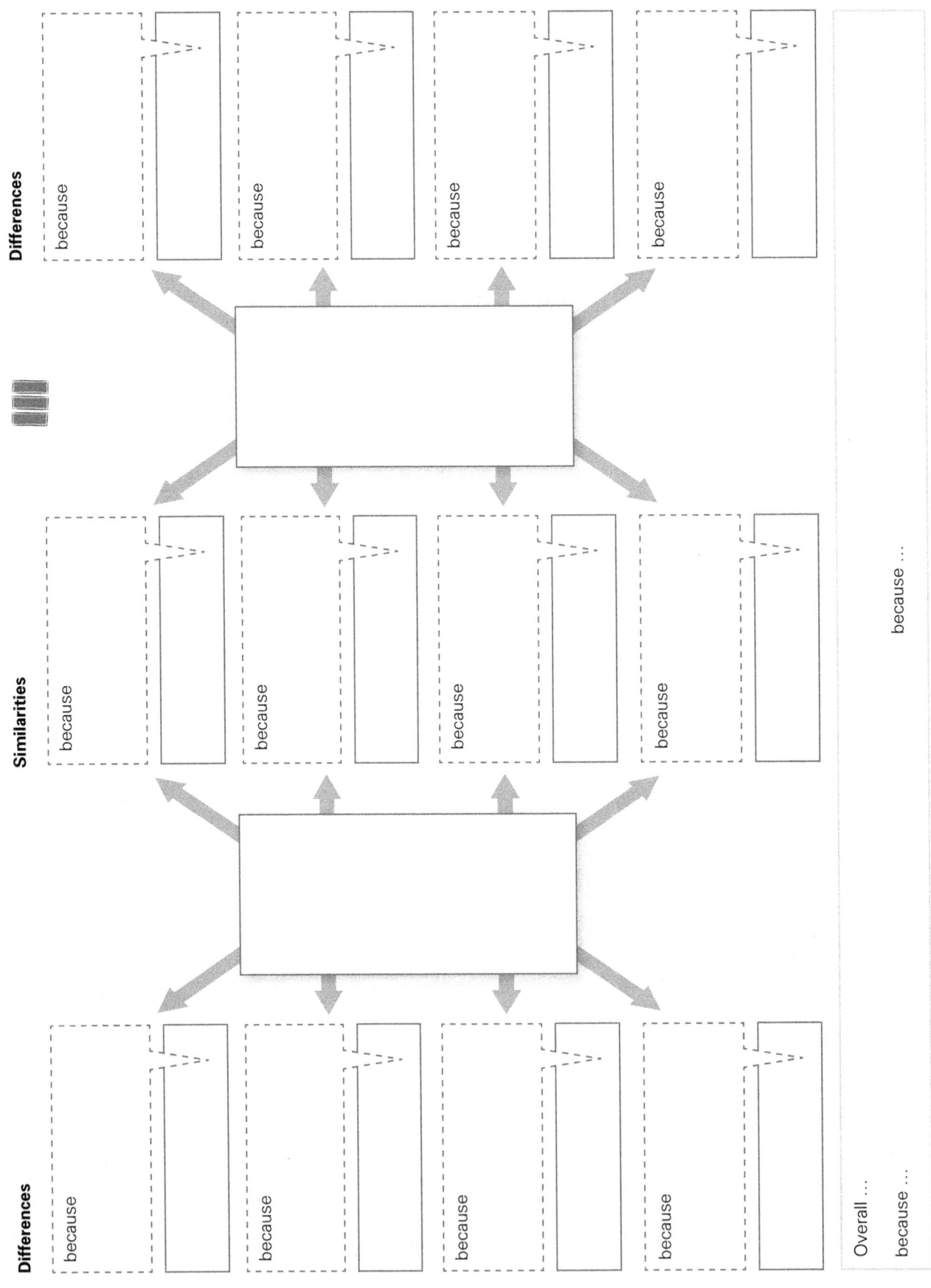

© Pam Hook and Julie Mills, 2011. All rights reserved

Note: For detailed instructions on using this map, see Hook and Mills (2011).

Template 2.3: HOT SOLO Compare and contrast self-assessment rubric

	... **and** I can make a generalisation ("Overall I think ...").	
	... **and** I can give reasons why ...	
	I can identify several relevant similarities and differences between [X] and [Y] ...	
	I can identify one relevant similarity and one relevant difference between [X] and [Y].	
	I can identify the objects/ideas but I need help to group them.	

SOLO learning log

My learning outcome is _____ because ...

My next step is to ...

© Pam Hook and Julie Mills, 2011. All rights reserved

Note: For detailed instructions on using this rubric, see Hook and Mills (2011).

Template 2.4: HookED SOLO reverse hexagons

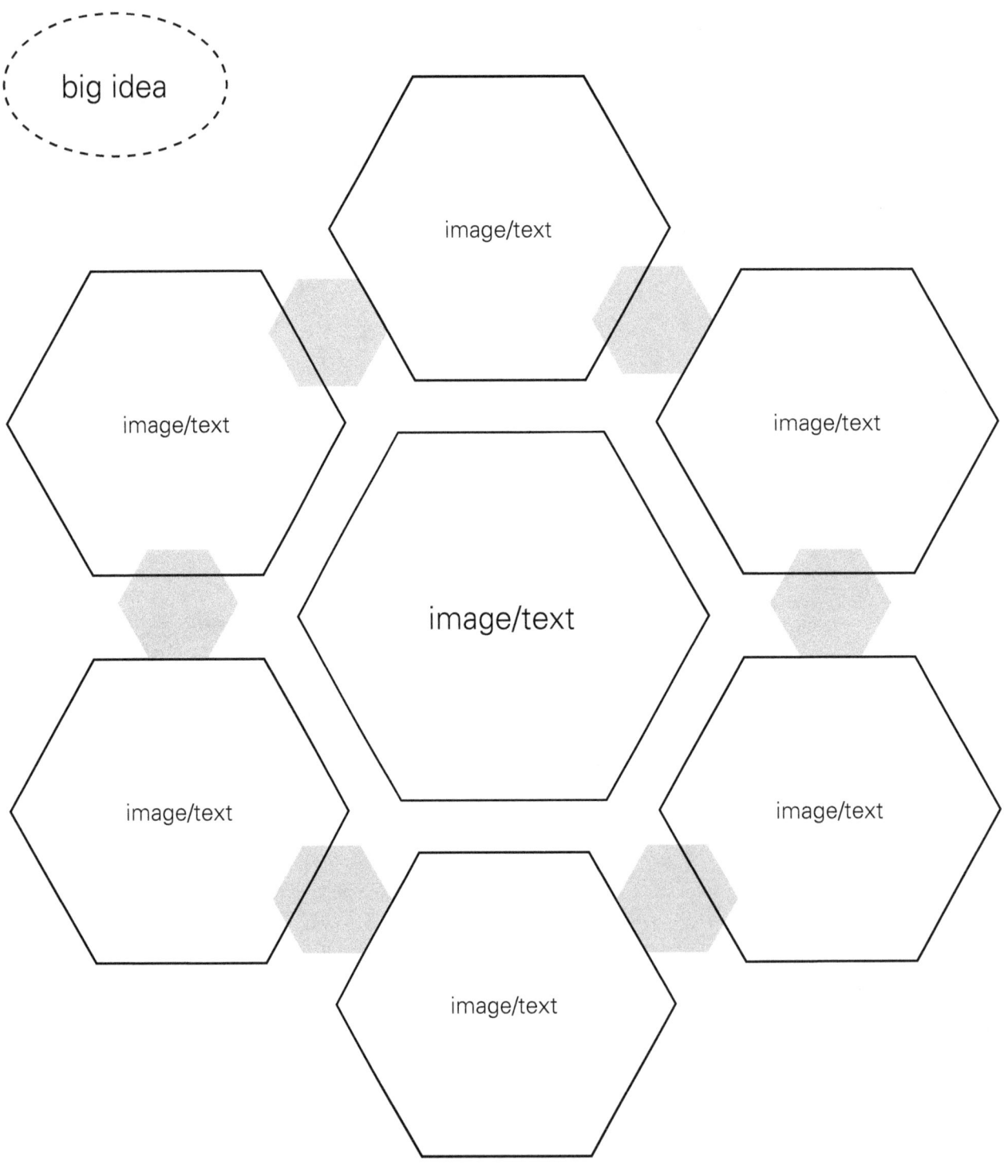

1. Identify each hexagon (unistructural).
2. Describe the content in each hexagon (multistructural).
3. Find the connections between individual hexagons (relational).
4. Make a generalisation about the big idea suggested by the hexagons (extended abstract).
5. Create a new hexagon to replace the central hexagon (extended abstract).
6. Make your own reverse hexagon template (extended abstract).

© Pam Hook, HookED, 2016. All rights reserved.

Exhibit 2.15: Example of student outcome using HookED SOLO reverse hexagons

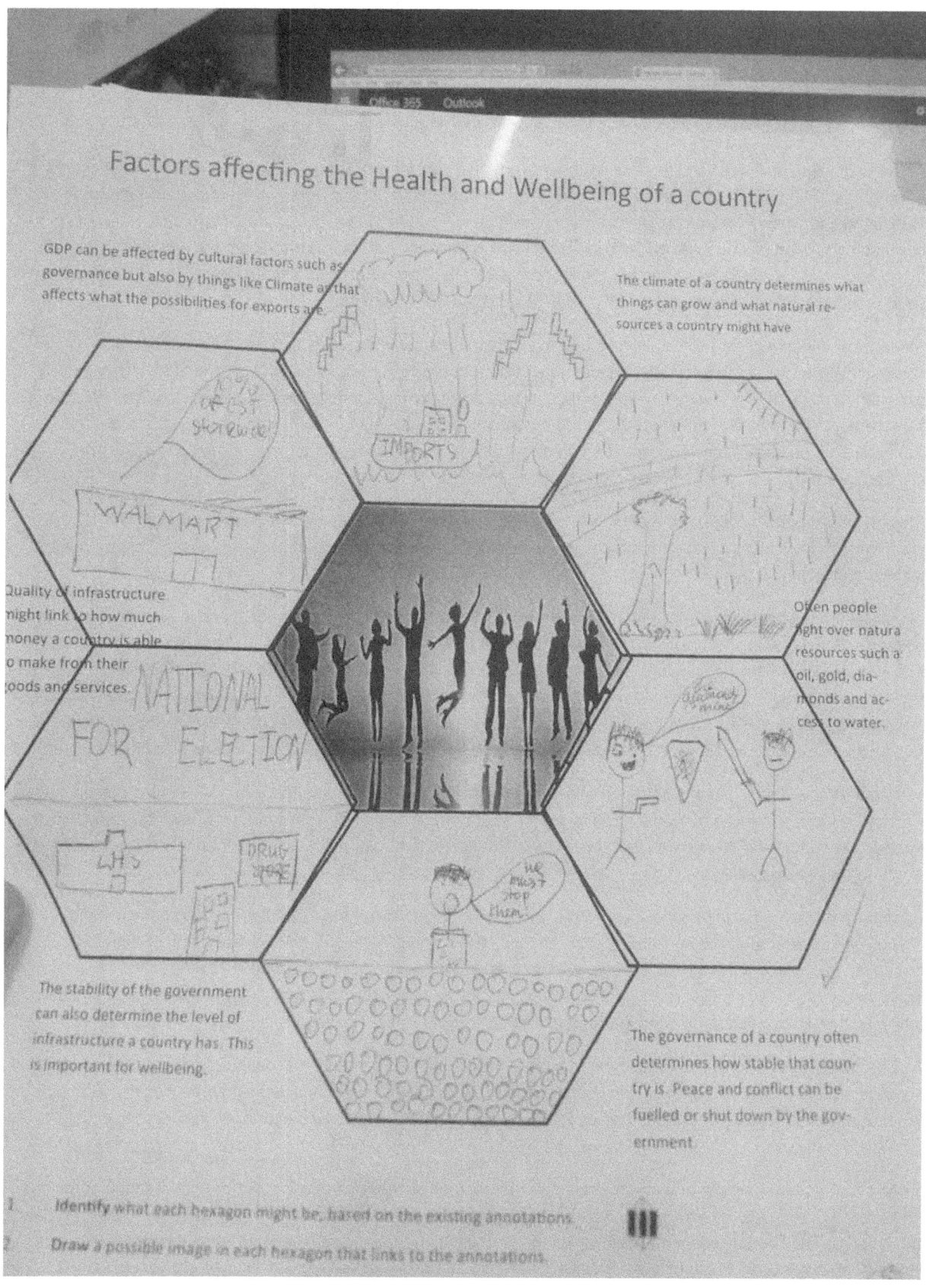

Source: Miriam Marshall, Lincoln High School

Community and SOLO

The third effective pedagogical approach identified by Aitken and Sinnema (2008) lies in building a learning community. This is achieved by promoting respectful and productive teacher–student and student–student relationships that focus on learning and how best to promote it.

In our experience of building learning communities, this process moves through several stages:

1. At the beginning, teachers and students struggle to create a common interpretation of learning and what counts as progress. Using SOLO as a shared model can help them to tease out and agree on what counts as evidence of learning and what counts as progress in the community. They spend time developing instruments, collecting baseline data, creating entry and exit tickets (identifying knowledge before and after learning) and responding to them, and so on. Teachers and students collect oodles of data. They often worry about how to make meaning from what they have collected and what meaning will be revealed from the data.

2. Students and teachers start to understand that every intervention will increase achievement and that, as a community, they must ask the powerful question, "What makes the greatest gain in achievement?" This is the explanation stage of community building. SOLO helps teachers and students explain the causes of their shifts in achievement. The SOLO-differentiated success criteria for "knowing about" and "knowing how to" show that achievement comes at many levels and that a next step will always follow, regardless of the complexity of a learning task.

3. Moving on to the next stage is challenging. It is easy to get stuck in reflection and inquiring into learning outcomes. In this stage, the community moves on to proactively monitor and act on strategies that create deep learning outcomes.

Relationships are important to community and communication is important to teacher/student and student/student relationships. Sharing a common language of learning through SOLO allows teachers and students to share interests, desired learning goals, next steps, feedback and feedforward, concerns and successes. The SOLO levels enable nuanced conversation about what I am doing, how well it is going and what I should do next. The levels allow students to elaborate on their level of "stuckedness". Teachers and students can collaborate when making decisions about what to do next – identifying those explicit, proximate and hierarchical next steps and working together to get the best learning outcome.

SOLO helps remove the sense of blame from learning communities and keeps the focus on the learning outcome. "My (or my student's) learning outcome has a relational structure for this task. What can I do to shift this structure to an extended abstract level?" Note also that the assessment sits with the structure of ideas in the learning outcome – it does not define the learner.

Community is built when students are empowered to make decisions about their own learning and participate in the design and assessment of their learning goals and success criteria. When students create a personalised SOLO-differentiated toolbox of strategies for bringing in, linking and/or extending ideas, they are empowered to make decisions about their learning. By coding strategies against SOLO levels, they can find the strategies that are most effective for them and rely less on direction from others:

> We build our own toolbox of strategies to bring in ideas, link ideas and extend ideas. Being able to choose my own strategies like the compare and contrast and explain causes map definitely helped me plan my writing. It helped me structure my ideas so I could answer the question. It gives you control over your own learning.
> (Year 11 student)

Involving students in constructing or co-constructing differentiated success criteria for their desired learning outcomes can include developing success criteria for a performance outcome like "building a learning community". Even primary school students can become adept at this task and use the resulting rubric to self- and peer-assess outcomes. Exhibit 2.16 presents an example of a self-assessment rubric for building a learning community. However, it is preferable that social sciences teachers and their students use this only as a scaffold to start the conversation from which they ultimately co-construct a SOLO rubric of their own. Early in this process they should also identify criteria that matter for "community" and "learning".

Exhibit 2.16: SOLO self-assessment rubric for building a learning community (knowing how to)

Learning intention [verb] [content] [context]	**Prestructural** *Needs help*	**Unistructural** *If directed*	**Multistructural** *Aware but no reasons, makes mistakes*	**Relational** *Purposeful, strategic, identifies and self-corrects mistakes*	**Extended abstract** *Seeks feedback to improve, acts as role model, teaches others*
Build a collaborative, inclusive and supportive learning community, that has trust, respect and cooperation	I need help to build a learning community that can engage and motivate students. I need help to foster trust, respect and cooperation with and among students.	I try to use strategies to engage and motivate students if directed. I try to foster trust, respect and cooperation with and among students if shown what to do.	I can use strategies to engage and motivate students. I can foster trust, respect and cooperation with and among students. However, I am not sure how or why I am doing this and it only works some of the time.	I can use strategies to engage and motivate students. I can foster trust, respect and cooperation with and among students I can explain how and why I do this …	… **and** I seek feedback from students and peers on how I can improve the sense of collaboration and inclusion in the learning community.
Effective strategies					

3. SOLO strategies for developing declarative knowledge

SOLO helps you ... the relational thinking side of things helps me compare and contrast my ideas and I can see what to do next to show my work is at an excellence level. Student, Lincoln High School.

This section focuses on SOLO strategies that support students in developing declarative knowledge, or "knowing about", that will get them thinking like a social scientist. Specifically it outlines SOLO strategies to develop students' skills in observational, experimental, correlational and conceptual thinking. As in earlier sections, a wealth of student examples illustrates the success of these approaches.

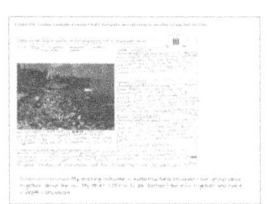
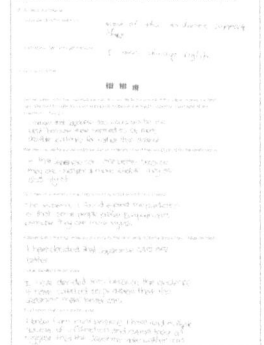

Observational thinking – description

Observation: What can you see or measure using the five senses?

Social scientists observe people. They record their behaviour in a systematic way using measurements and/or impressions. When you ask, "What is going on here?", you are thinking like a social scientist. To answer the question, students must undertake skilled and active descriptive analysis.

It tends to be easy to identify the attributes of a phenomenon: to ask and answer, "What is it like? What are the attributes?" For students thinking like social scientists, it is more challenging to identify the important attributes of a phenomenon because, to determine relative importance, they must make links between ideas. Justifying the importance of attributes is a relational or deep thinking outcome, which may involve:

- finding reasons for or contributing causes (*explain causes*) of different attributes
- identifying similarities (*classify*)
- identifying similarities and differences (*compare and contrast*).

Finally, students must step back and look at the wider implications. They must tease out conceptual understandings of their description through part–whole analysis and generalisation.

Exhibit 3.1 summarises the different skills involved in a descriptive analysis and identifies helpful SOLO strategies to support each stage.

Some SOLO-based strategies that support student description are the HookED SOLO Describe ++ map and self-assessment rubric (Templates 3.1 and 3.2). A SOLO multi-level map, Describe ++ is sometimes called "the one map to rule them all". Exhibit 3.2 shows how prompts in a HookED SOLO Describe ++ map deepened a student's response when they described a social action based on the Sea Shepherd Conservation Society, in answer to:

> What is this organisation trying to do to help people or the environment? What are the social actions they are doing and how effective are these actions?

Exhibit 3.1: Skills and supporting SOLO strategies in a descriptive analysis

Attributes			
Characteristics related to an idea (*describe*)	Grouped on the basis of similarities (*classify*)	Grouped on the basis of similarities or differences (*compare and contrast*)	Sorted in terms of their influence on the whole (*analyse part–whole*)
Supporting SOLO strategies			
HookED SOLO Describe ++ map and self-assessment rubric	HOT SOLO Classify map and self-assessment rubric	HOT SOLO Compare and contrast map and self-assessment rubric	HOT SOLO Analyse part–whole map and self-assessment rubric
			HOT SOLO Generalise map and self-assessment rubric

Exhibit 3.2: Student use of a HookED SOLO Describe ++ map to describe a social action

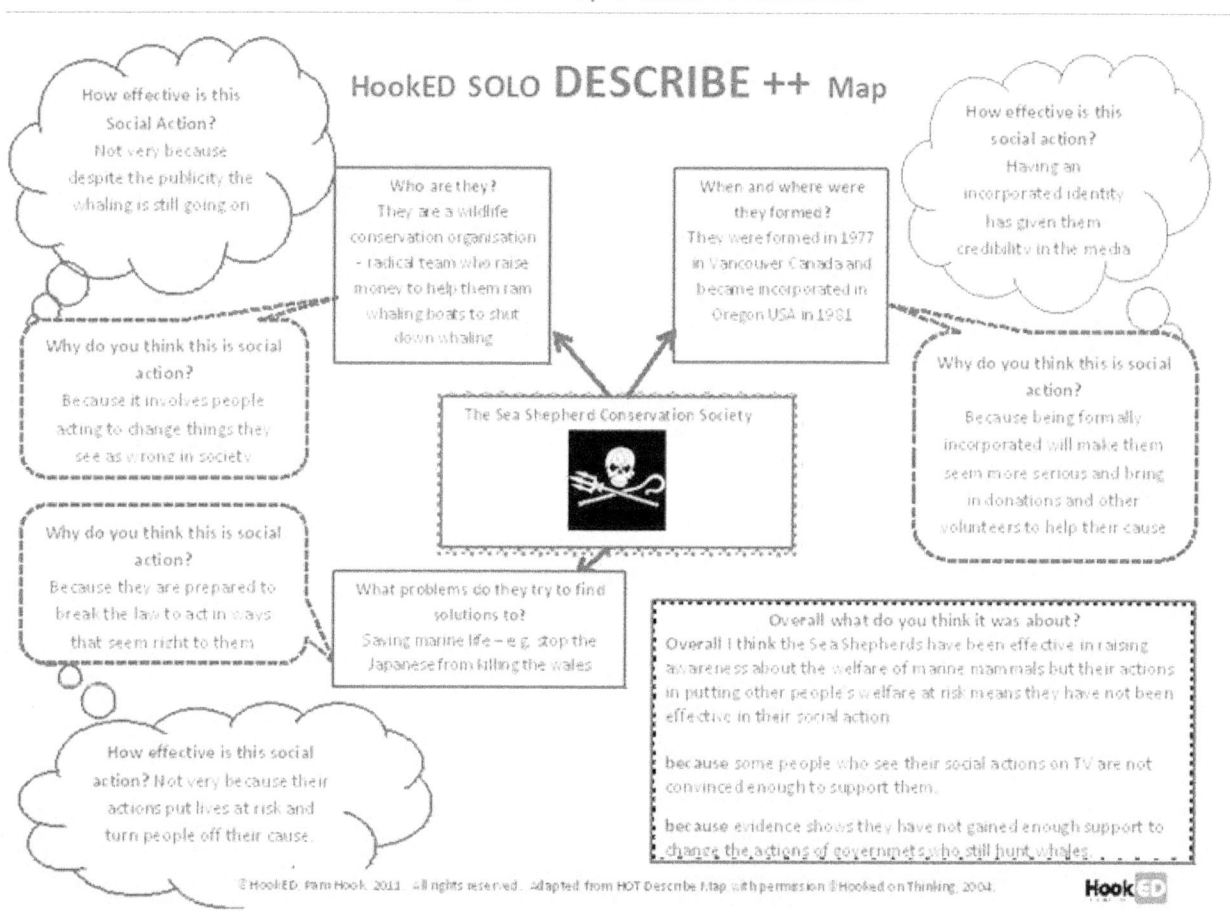

Template 3.1: HookED SOLO Describe ++ map

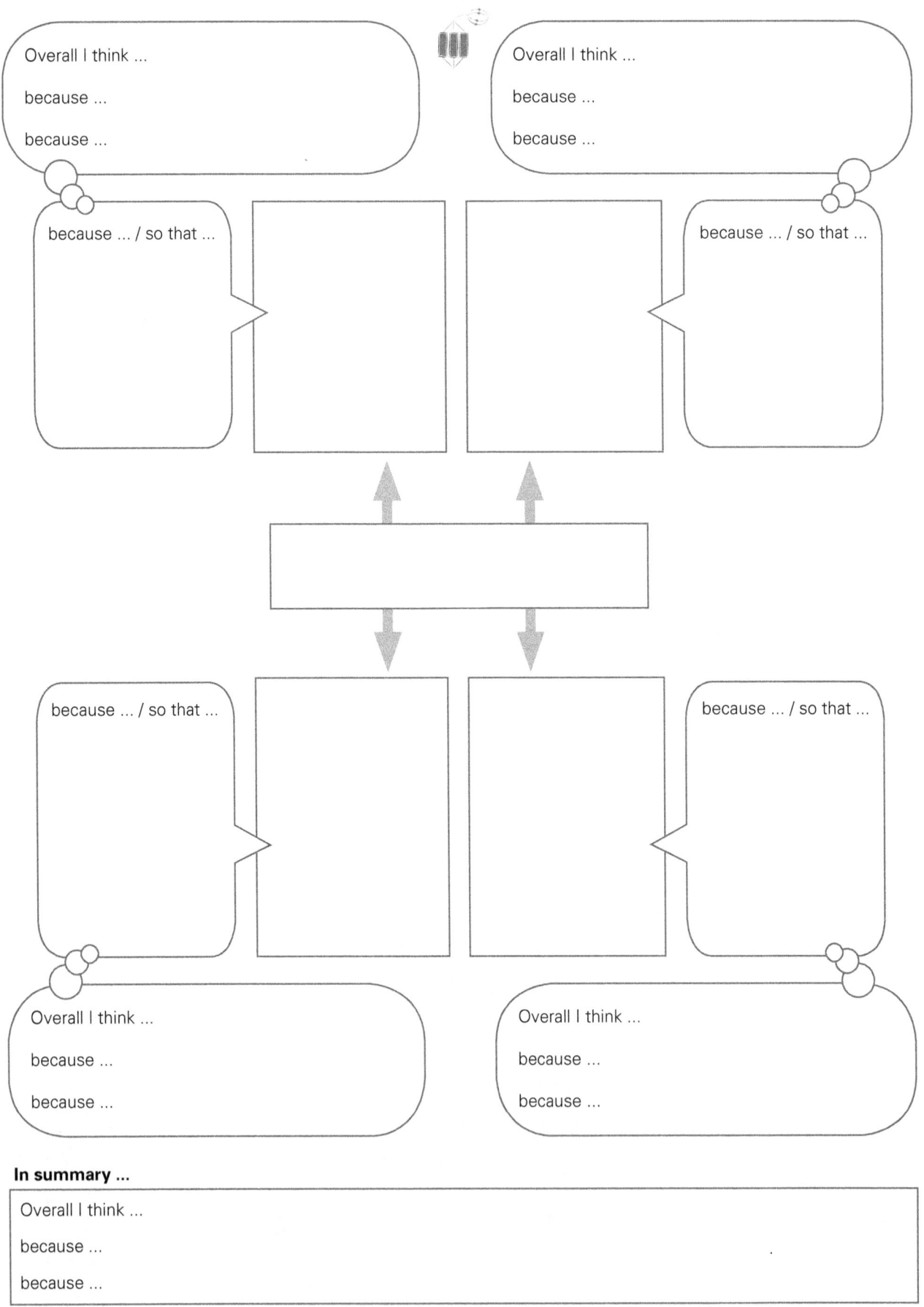

© Pam Hook, HookED, 2016. All rights reserved.

Note: For detailed instructions on using this map, see Hook (2015).

Template 3.2: HookED SOLO Describe ++ self-assessment rubric

SOLO level	Learning outcome	
Extended abstract		My description identifies several relevant features, links these and makes a generalisation. It integrates these generalisations into a new understanding.
Relational		My description identifies several relevant features and links these by explanation.
Multistructural		My description identifies several relevant features.
Unistructural		My description identifies one relevant feature.
Prestructural		I need help to identify any relevant features.

SOLO learning log

My learning outcome is _____ because …

My next step is to …

© Pam Hook, HookED, 2016. All rights reserved.

Note: For detailed instructions on using this map, see Hook (2015).

Experimental thinking – causality and making inferences

> Inference: What can you infer from what you observe?

Inferences explain what we observe and/or measure. To infer is to make a claim drawn from evidence and to reason about what we already know; it involves retrospective thinking about an observation.

Social scientists try to determine causality, asking, "What is really happening and why? Is variable *x* a cause of *y*?" The causal mechanism can vary. Students may assume that the most likely mechanism is that variable *x* causes *y*, thinking that events of type *x* are always followed by events of type *y*. But in some circumstances, *x* may be a necessary but not sufficient condition for *y*. It is possible that *x* causes *y* but a chain of causal mechanisms comes between the two. It is possible that the existence of *x* merely increases the likelihood of *y*.

Causes can be singular or multiple, generic or idiosyncratic. Causal explanation may look at the individual, local or global level, with all of these perspectives relying on comparative analysis to determine causation. For example, as the result of social protests, a government regime may be overthrown or that regime may increase its repressive measures; increasing use of technology and outsourcing, reduced wages and economic recession are multiple and interdependent causes of strike action and social unrest.

For students wanting to think like social scientists, the challenge is to identify and then justify a claim for causality. Part of this skill is to distinguish between correlation and causality. Just because two events seem to vary in similar ways does not prove a relationship exists, as the website Spurious Correlations (**www.tylervigen.com**) affirms.

The HookED SOLO Explain causes map and self-assessment rubric (Templates 3.3 and 3.4) offer a strategy to help students think about causal explanations from multiple perspectives – what causes, conditions or circumstances combined to bring the outcome about? With this scaffolding, students can test and justify an inference.

Exhibit 3.3 presents an example of a student's use of the map to explain the causes of Japanese youth cultures. The conclusion shows the student using information in a new way by comparing Japan to other countries. In addition they make generalisations and link to concepts like "fashion" (see the next section on correlational thinking).

Exhibit 3.3: Student use of a HookED SOLO Explain causes map to explain the causes of Japanese youth cultures

Sub-cultures are all over the world. But we all copy what other people or countries do. We take ideas from different cultures, we look at what people did in the past and we create new, 'original' sub-cultures. So Japan may have some weird sub-cultures but they would have gotten ideas from people in different countries. And that is exactly what we do too. There isn't really such a thing as an original idea or thought. In fact fashion is a big example of this. We may think that what we are wearing today is the 'new' trend, when really our parents used to wear similar stuff at our age. Overall Japanese sub-cultures are different but not original because there isn't really such a thing as an original thought because everyone just takes ideas from each other.

Template 3.3: HookED SOLO Explain causes map

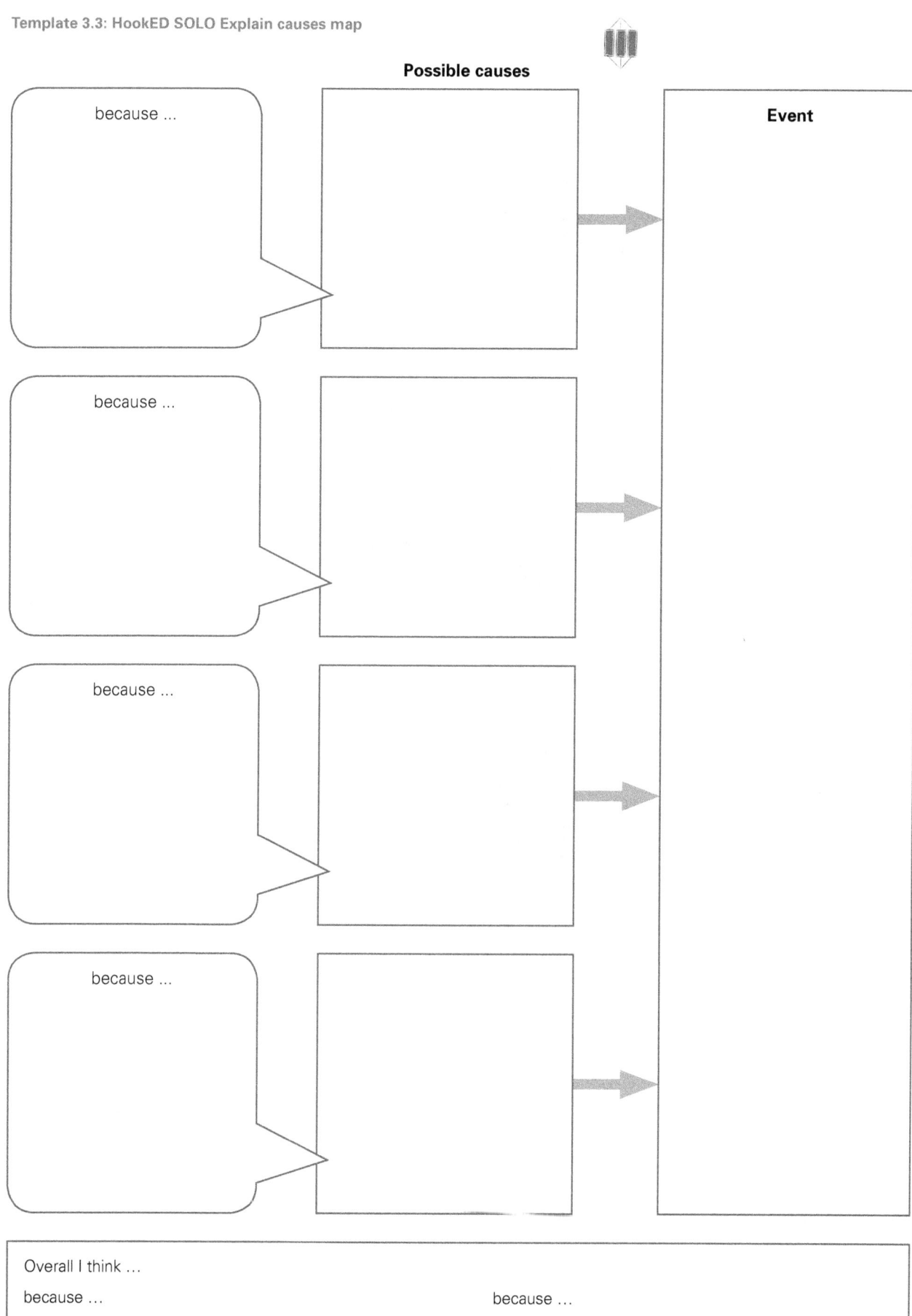

Overall I think ...

because ... because ...

© Pam Hook, HookED, 2016. All rights reserved.

Note: For detailed instructions on using this map, see Hook (2015).

Template 3.4: HookED SOLO Explain causes self-assessment rubric

SOLO level	Learning outcome	
Extended abstract		... **and** I look at it in a new way.
Relational		... **and** I explain how the causes relate to the event ...
Multistructural		I identify the event and several relevant causes of the event ...
Unistructural		I identify the event and one relevant cause of the event.
Prestructural		I identify the event but need help to identify the causes of the event.

SOLO learning log

My learning outcome is _____ because ...

My next step is to ...

© Pam Hook, HookED, 2016. All rights reserved.

Note: For detailed instructions on using this rubric, see Hook (2015).

Correlational thinking – prediction

> Prediction: What do you predict will happen next?

Social scientists make predictions based on what they observe. Predictions extend what we observe or measure to a future that is yet to be determined. To predict is to make a claim about things that are not already known – prospective or forward-looking thinking.

When social scientists make predictions, it is because they have not or cannot establish the truth by a more direct method like direct observation or experiment. Prediction is always risky. For students wanting to think like social scientists, the challenge lies in the complexity of human behaviour: its many interdependent causes limit the reliability of prediction in the social sciences.

The HOT SOLO Predict map and self-assessment rubric offer a strategy to help students test and justify a prediction (Templates 3.5 and 3.6).

Exhibit 3.4 presents a student's predictions about Japanese cars, made with the scaffolding of a HOT SOLO Predict map. The value of the SOLO approach is clearly demonstrated in Exhibit 3.5, which contrasts a student's predictions made with and without SOLO Predict map scaffolding.

Exhibit 3.4: Student example of using a HOT SOLO Predict map to make predictions about Japanese cars

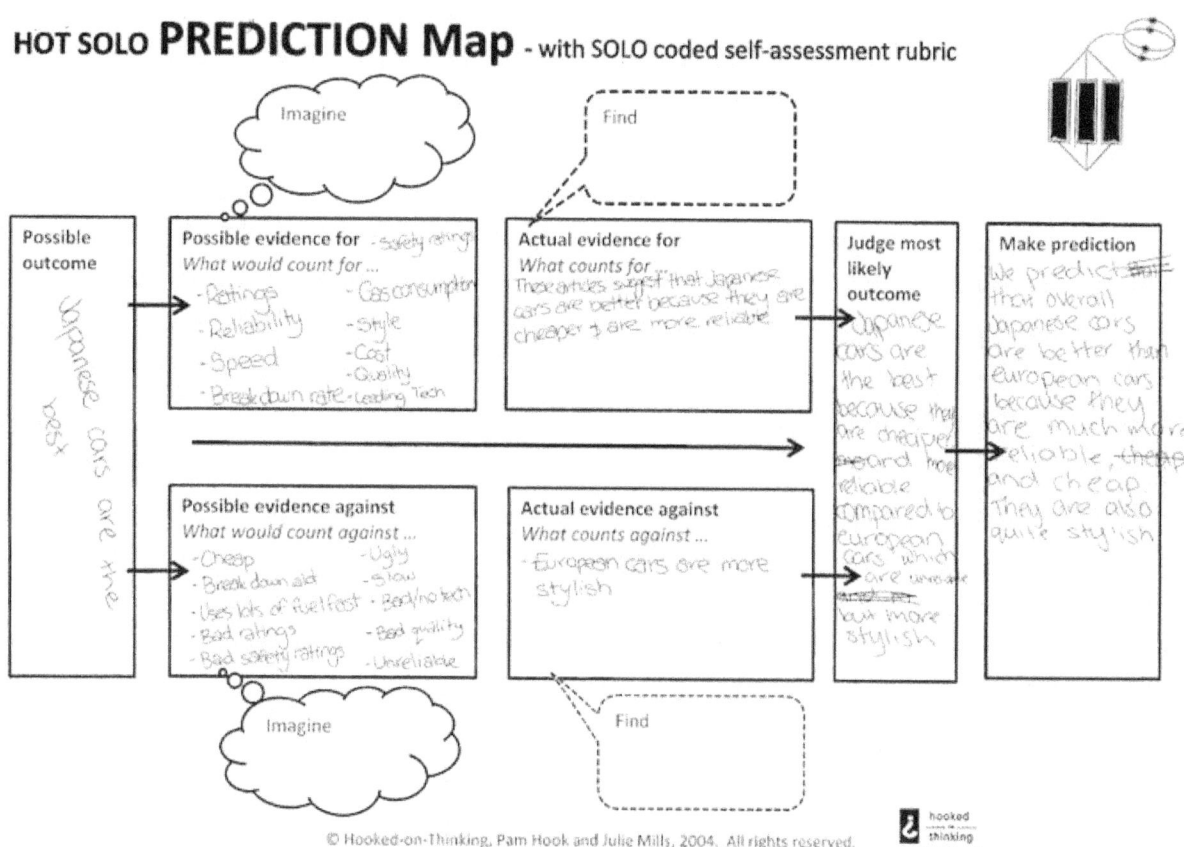

Exhibit 3.5: Student examples of writing a prediction with and without the scaffolding of the HOT SOLO Predict map

(a) Without scaffolding

I have decided this because …

most of the evidence supports this

And I know that I am right because …

I am always right

(b) With scaffolding

Before researching the Japanese car industry, we made the prediction that Japan makes the best cars. We then thought about some possible evidence that would support or count against this prediction. I thought …

I thought that Japanese cars would still be the best because there seemed to be more possible evidence for rather than against.

We then looked for actual evidence. Actual evidence I found that would count for the prediction is …

Is that Japanese cars are better because they are cheaper & more reliable. They are also stylish.

With regard to evidence that might count against the prediction, I found …

The evidence I found against the prediction is that some people prefer European cars because they are more stylish.

Following this thinking, in terms of clarifying the most likely outcome (prediction), I have decided …

I have decided that Japanese cars are better.

I have decided this because …

I have decided this because the evidence I have collected says overall that the Japanese make better cars.

And I know that I am right because …

I know I am right because I have read multiple sources of information and overall they all suggest that the Japanese make better cars.

Template 3.5: HOT SOLO Predict map

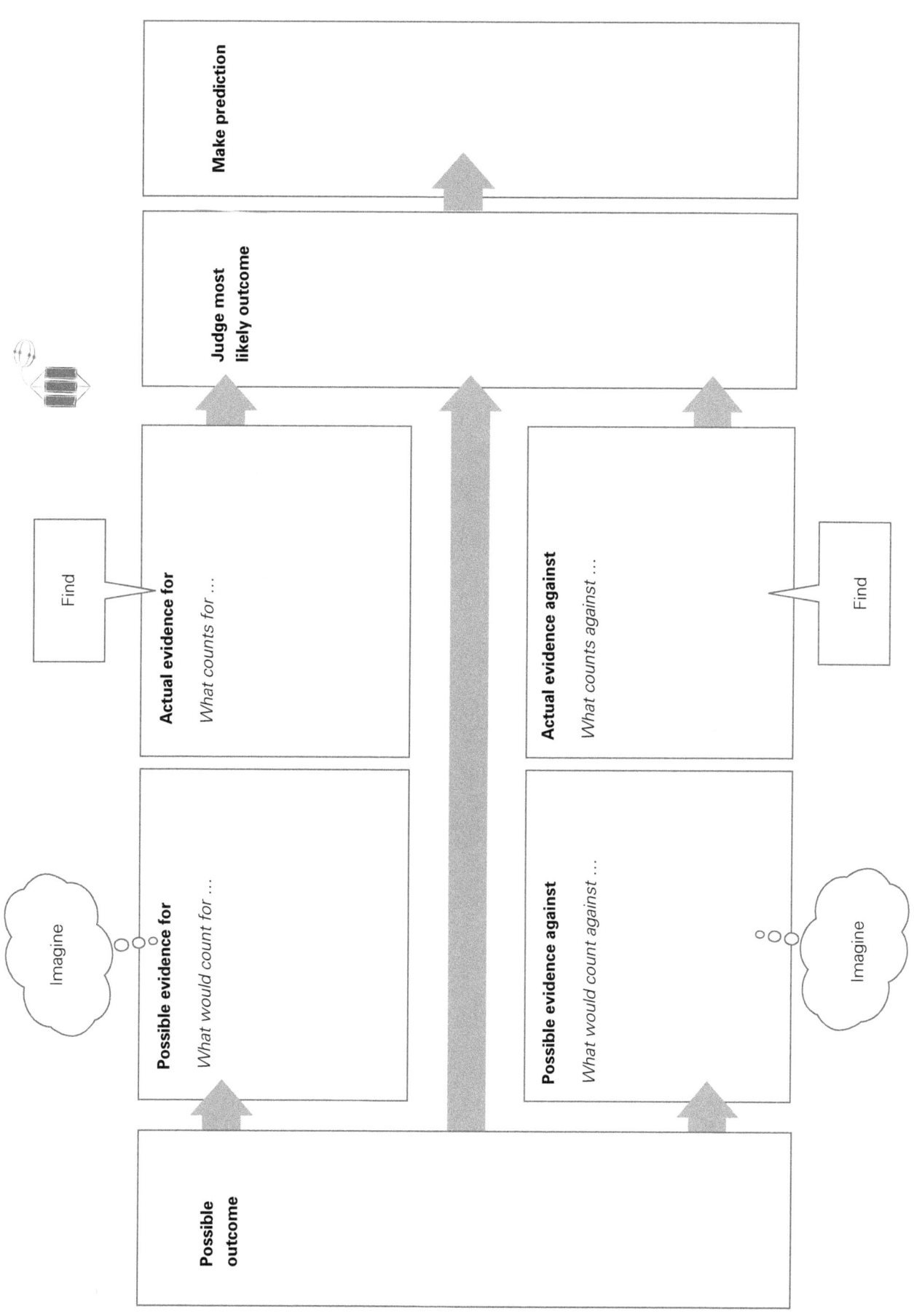

© Pam Hook and Julie Mills, 2011. All rights reserved.

Note: For detailed instructions on using this map, see Hook and Mills (2011).

Template 3.6: HOT SOLO Predict self-assessment rubric

	... **and** I can: • find evidence to support and/or reject the outcome • judge the likeliness of the outcome • make a prediction.	
	... **and** I can explain why this evidence would support or reject the outcome ...	
	I can suggest several pieces of evidence needed to support or reject the possible outcome ...	
	I can suggest evidence needed to support or reject the possible outcome.	
	I need help to test a possible outcome.	

SOLO learning log

My learning outcome is _____ because ...

My next step is to ...

© Pam Hook and Julie Mills, 2011. All rights reserved.

Note: For detailed instructions on using this rubric, see Hook and Mills (2011).

Conceptual thinking – generalising

> Generalising: What insightful conclusions can you draw?

Social phenomena often cannot be directly observed or quantified under controlled conditions. Social scientists often need to indirectly explore social phenomena by analysing individual and group motivation and behaviour, and their effects on institutions, and then generalise about the concepts, values and perspectives involved.

Making generalisations is a SOLO extended abstract task. It requires students to think in a new way – to extend their thinking. To do this, they make a claim, elaborate on it, give reasons for it, and provide evidence of its reliability and validity. This structure remains the same whether students are drawing conclusions based on concepts, points of view, values, perspectives or insight. The student examples that follow cover all of these areas.

Generalising based on concepts – "The big idea is …"

The HOT SOLO Generalise map and self-assessment rubric (Templates 3.7 and 3.8) offer an effective strategy to support students' conceptual thinking and make its structure visible.

Social sciences concepts include many big ideas, ranging from change, place and space to sustainability and globalisation, to processes and patterns. One way of encouraging deep or higher-order thinking across the social sciences is to prompt students to integrate conceptual understandings into any given context using a SOLO Integrate concepts map, in which they:

- identify the conceptual link (unistructural task)
- explain why the picture is linked to the concept (relational task)
- draw a conclusion about the picture and the links (extended abstract task).

Exhibit 3.6 presents a student's work produced through this process and their self-assessment of it.

Exhibit 3.6: Student example of using a SOLO Integrate concepts map to develop conceptual thinking

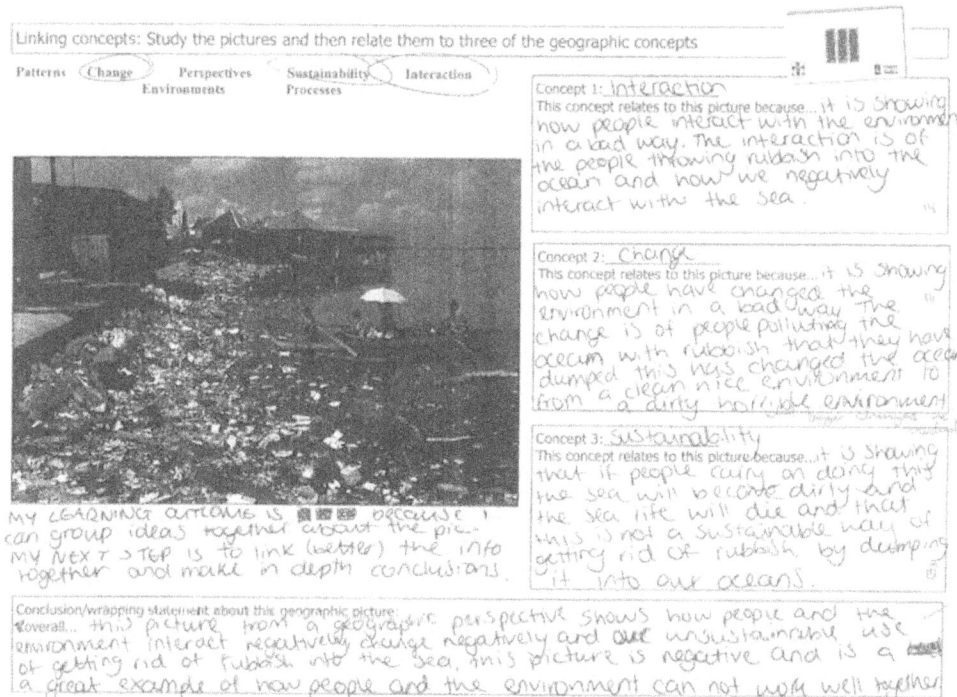

Student self-assessment: My learning outcome is multistructural because I can group ideas together about the pic. My NEXT STEP is to link (better) the info together and make in depth conclusions.

Template 3.7: HOT SOLO Generalise map

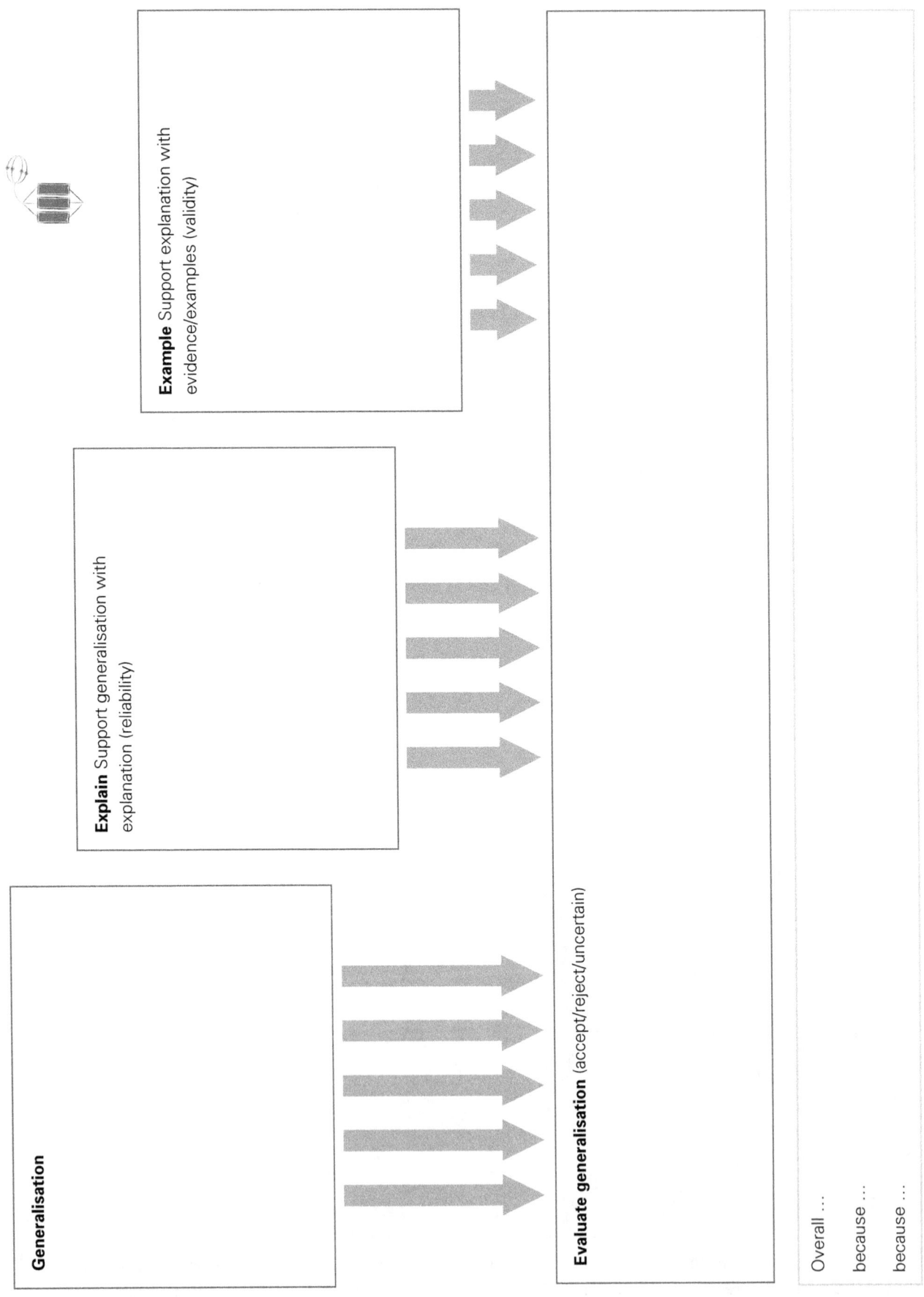

© Pam Hook and Julie Mills, 2011. All rights reserved.

Note: For detailed instructions on using this map, see Hook and Mills (2011).

Template 3.8: HOT SOLO Generalise self-assessment rubric

	... **and** I can: • provide evidence to support it • evaluate the generalisation.	
	... **and** I can provide reasons to support it ...	
	... **and** I can clarify its meaning ...	
	I can make a generalisation ...	
	I need help to make a generalisation.	

SOLO learning log

My learning outcome is _____ because ...

My next step is to ...

© Pam Hook and Julie Mills, 2011. All rights reserved.

Note: For detailed instructions on using this rubric, see Hook and Mills (2011).

Generalising based on points of view – "I think that …"

Points of view are the opinions individuals express and the actions they take on particular social issues. SOLO helps differentiate the social inquiry task when students are exploring points of view.

For example, the SOLO-coded map in Exhibit 3.7 helped Year 9 students conduct social inquiry into the varied points of view and values held by Māori and Europeans during early European settlement in New Zealand.[1] With the SOLO maps, they explored the different points of view expressed when one group (pre-European Māori) valued the wellbeing of the collective and the other (European settlers) valued individual wellbeing. The teacher and the map's designer, Rachel Meadowcroft, reported that students liked using this map, along with the SOLO Value exploration map (see below) because it helped them understand the task and made the learning outcomes visible and easier to achieve.

Exhibit 3.7: SOLO Points of view questions and map focusing on early European settlement in New Zealand

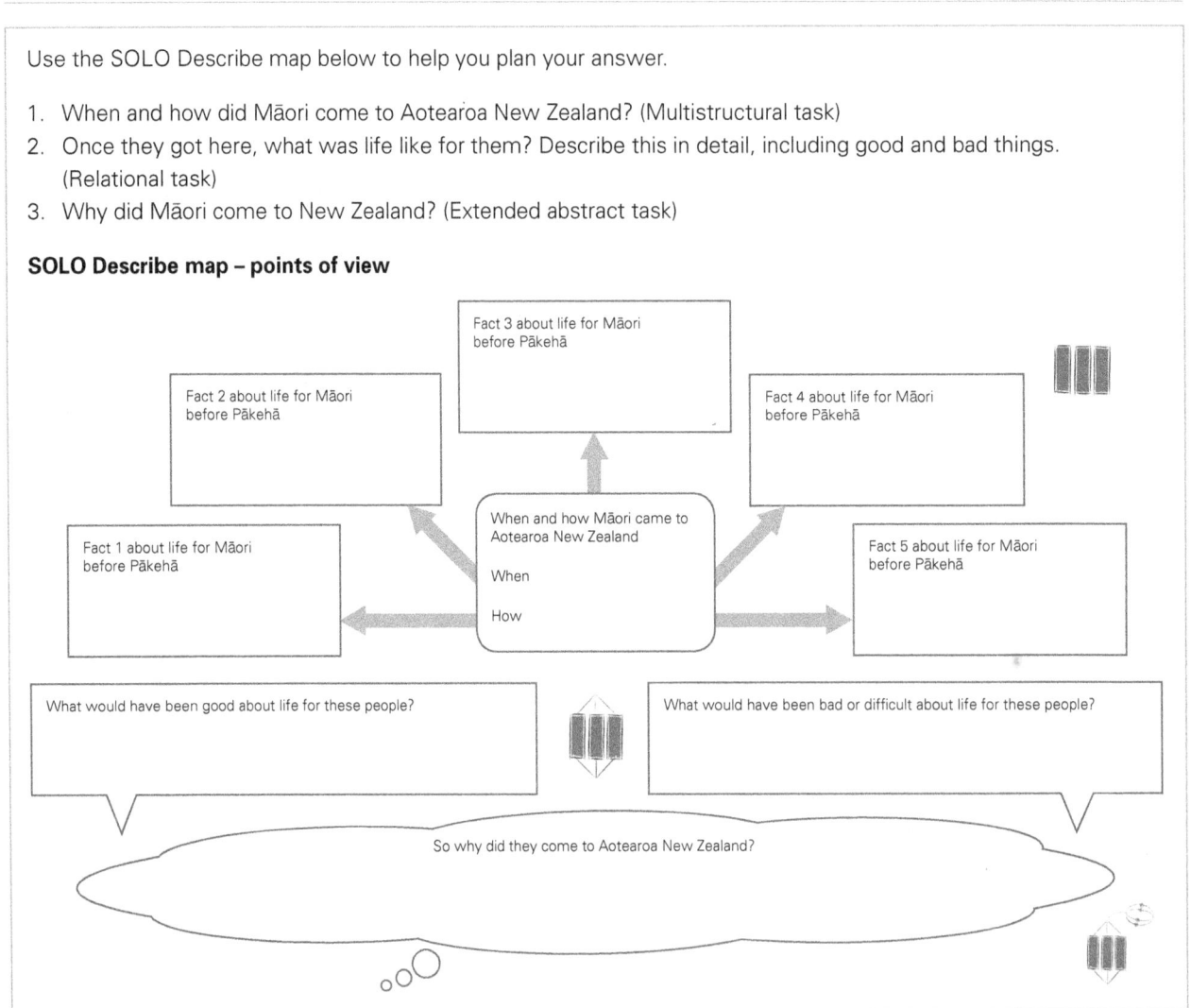

Source: Rachel Meadowcroft, Lincoln High School

Generalising based on values – "Why I hold this point of view …"

Values are deeply held beliefs and understandings that individuals, groups and communities hold about what is important. They are the expressions that explain "why I hold this point of view". People can have strikingly different moral, social, cultural, aesthetic, economic and environmental beliefs. These differences help explain how different groups of people see the world and social phenomena in markedly different ways.

---

1 In early Māori society, individual identity was seen in collective terms through whānau (extended family), hapū (subtribe) and iwi (tribe). The European settlers valued autonomous individuality. These different perspectives ultimately affected land ownership, when collectively held land was transferred into individual titles and then to individual European land owners.

Asking students to position themselves along a values continuum is an effective way of showing them how they differ in their opinions about the importance of values like power, fairness, equality, justice, peace, family, love, safety, helping others, doing what's right, adventure, friendship, land, wealth, freedom and/or survival.

As the above discussion on points of view shows, SOLO is useful in designing differentiated prompts to help students explore the points of view of individuals, groups and communities. With SOLO, they can explore these points of view more deeply and identify the values that might lie behind a particular point of view. Exhibit 3.8 continues on from the exploration of points of view during the time of early European settlement in New Zealand, showing how a SOLO map prompted students to explore different values as well.

Exhibit 3.8: SOLO Points of view and values questions and map focusing on early European settlement in New Zealand

Think more deeply about the point of view of early Māori settlers in Aotearoa by answering these questions in as much detail as you can. Use the SOLO Points of view and values map below to help you plan your answer.

1. How do you think they would have felt about their new life? Include at least two different things they would have been feeling and thinking. (Multistructural task)
2. Why would they have felt like this? Give as many detailed reasons as you can. (Relational task)
3. What values do you think were important to them? How do you know this? (Relational task)
4. How do you think Māori would have felt when Pākehā settlers began arriving? Why would they have felt like this? Give as many detailed reasons as you can. (Extended abstract task)

SOLO Points of view and values exploration map

Source: Rachel Meadowcroft, Lincoln High School

Generalising based on perspectives – "From my perspective ..."

Perspectives are informed by people's values; scientific, cultural, social justice, economic, indigenous, educational and medical perspectives are just a few examples. They are "world views" or "umbrella terms". It is possible if not probable that individuals can hold several perspectives on one issue.

Spatial and ecological perspectives are central to thinking like a social scientist. Historians exercise a temporal–spatial perspective when they ask, "When did it happen? What happened before and after?" Geographers look at space and place from a spatial perspective to ask, "Where is it? Why is it there?" From an ecological perspective, social scientists ask, "How is this phenomenon connected to the network of living and non-living things found in ecosystems?"

Because of the great number and variety of perspectives, students can feel overwhelmed by choice, struggling to know where to start. The SOLO Perspectives map (Exhibit 3.9) helps slow down and clarify students' thinking about perspectives. They can think carefully and deliberately about each prompt for multistructural, relational and extended abstract thinking.

Exhibit 3.9: SOLO Perspectives map for clarifying and scaffolding student thinking about perspectives

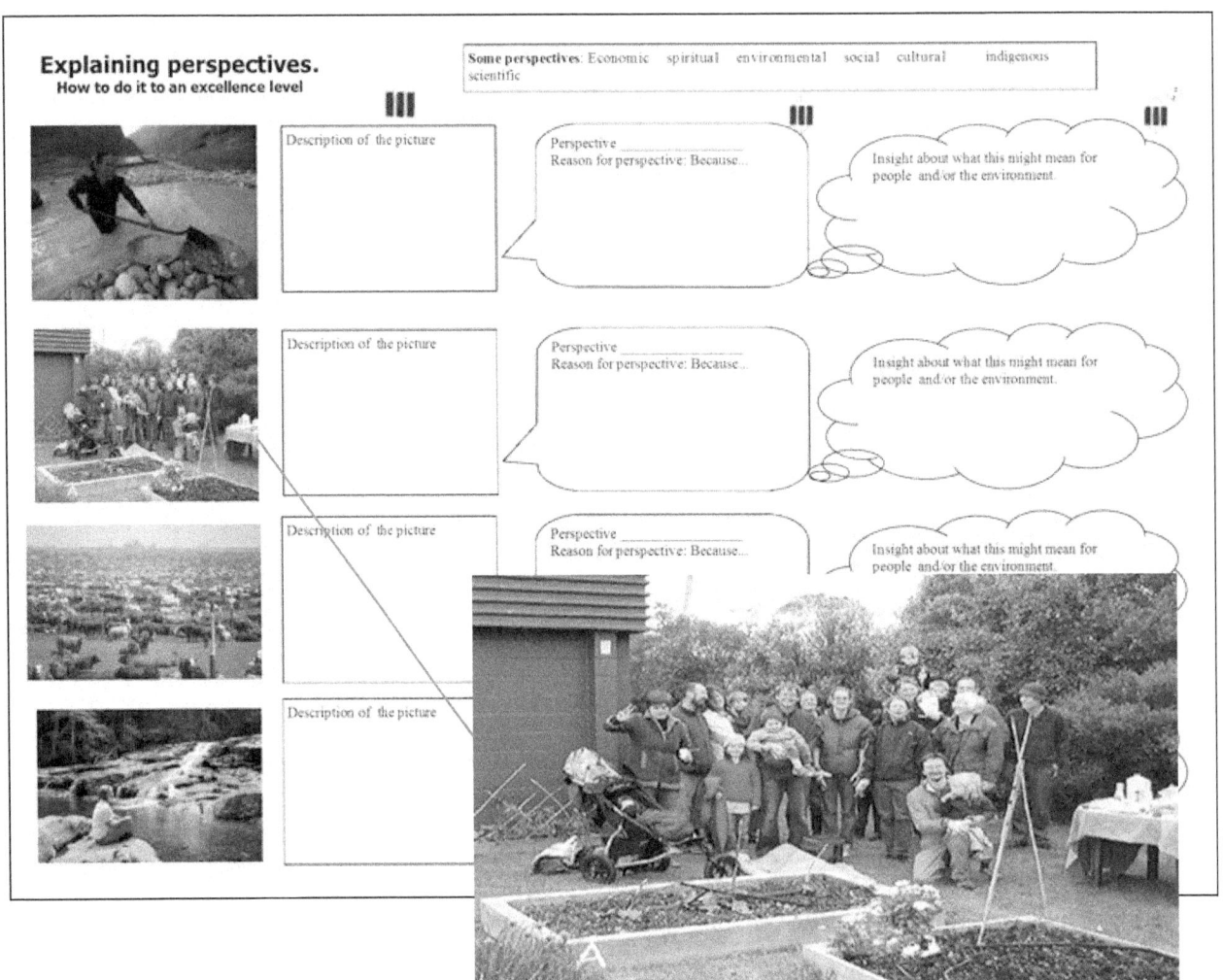

For example, when showing students the garden photograph from Exhibit 3.9, the teacher might describe the scene as showing:

> A group of people of varying ages, either in a cold climate or winter time. They seem to be happy. In the foreground are garden plots. A table has what looks to be food on it.

Then when making links to the various perspectives on the map, the teacher might say:

> A **social perspective** might apply to this setting as it looks like a number of families have come together to be part of what might be a community garden where they have all shared in being part of a bigger group project.

Looking for insight, the teacher might suggest:

> **Insight**, or using this information in a new way, might include predicting that this will be a resilient community and, if faced with an extreme event like an earthquake, they will band together and cope better than communities that do not have common social connections.

Generalising based on insight

To show insight, students need to think beyond what is known; to think at an extended abstract level. We often look for insight from an identified perspective or context, as in Exhibit 3.10.

Exhibit 3.10: SOLO self-assessment visual rubric for generalising based on insight

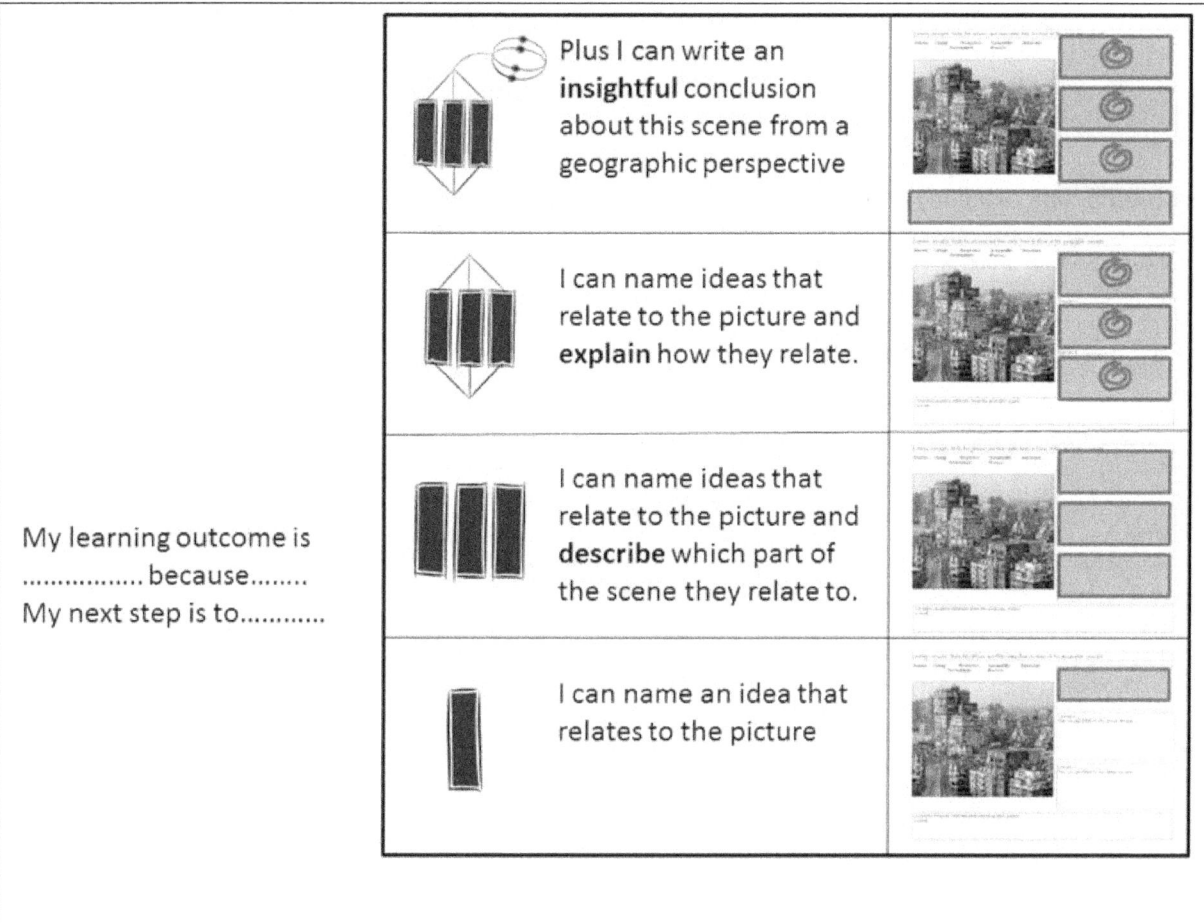

To develop insight, students:

- evaluate the strengths and weaknesses of the quantitative and qualitative evidence available
- clarify the nature of any causal relationships
- identify unwarranted assumptions and inferences
- determine whose voice is amplified and whose is not heard
- draw conclusions, from all of the above, about the influence of different perspectives on decisions made and actions taken.

When we look at quantitative and qualitative evidence in the social sciences, we are interested in its validity: does the evidence show what it claims to show (Goodman 2008)?

To show insight, students can ask:

- How was the evidence collected? Does the way the data were collected measure what it is meant to measure? If we used this method of collecting evidence again, would we get similar results? (Is the measure reliable?)
- What can we infer from the evidence? What assumptions do we make when we make these inferences? To what extent are these assumptions warranted or unwarranted?
- Is there a causal relationship between the variables under study or are some other factors at play?
- Can the results from the study population be generalised to the wider population?
- Does the way the evidence was collected fit with the real world?

Note:

- An **assumption** is something we do not question; something we take for granted. It is a prior belief – something established previously.
- An **inference** that something is true is based on something else being true. It is often based on prior beliefs or assumptions.

Although finding insight is well supported by the HookED Describe ++ map process, it is also possible to separate the tasks and make each one separately visible using SOLO strategies (Exhibit 3.11).

Exhibit 3.11: SOLO strategies to support the separate tasks that contribute to finding insight

Task contributing to finding insight	Supporting SOLO strategies
1. Evaluate strengths and weaknesses of evidence	HOT SOLO Evaluate map and self-assessment rubric (Hook and Mills 2011)
2. Clarify the nature of any causal relationships	HookED SOLO Explain causes map and self-assessment rubric (Templates 3.3 and 3.4)
3. Identify unwarranted assumptions and inferences	HookED SOLO Describe ++ map and self-assessment rubric (Templates 3.1 and 3.2)
4. Determine whose voice is amplified and whose is not heard	HOT SOLO Generalise map and self-assessment rubric (Templates 3.7 and 3.8)
5. Draw conclusions about the influence of different perspectives on decisions made and actions taken	HOT SOLO Generalise map and self-assessment rubric (Templates 3.7 and 3.8)

4. SOLO strategies for developing functioning knowledge

When students say, "I can't do this because I cannot draw", we need to hear them having actually said, "I need help identifying effective strategies for success". SOLO rubrics make this type of thinking visible. C Perry, geography teacher

This section focuses on SOLO strategies that support students in developing functioning knowledge, or "knowing how to", that will get them thinking like a social scientist. Specifically it identifies some key SOLO strategies to develop students' skills in interpreting and constructing resources, as well as their communication, social and fieldwork skills.

Interpreting resources

The following HOT SOLO Describe self-assessment visual rubrics support students in interpreting a resource when they need to:

- describe a global pattern (Exhibit 4.1)
- describe how and why people use the environment (Exhibit 4.2).

Exhibit 4.1: HOT SOLO Describe self-assessment visual rubric for describing a global pattern

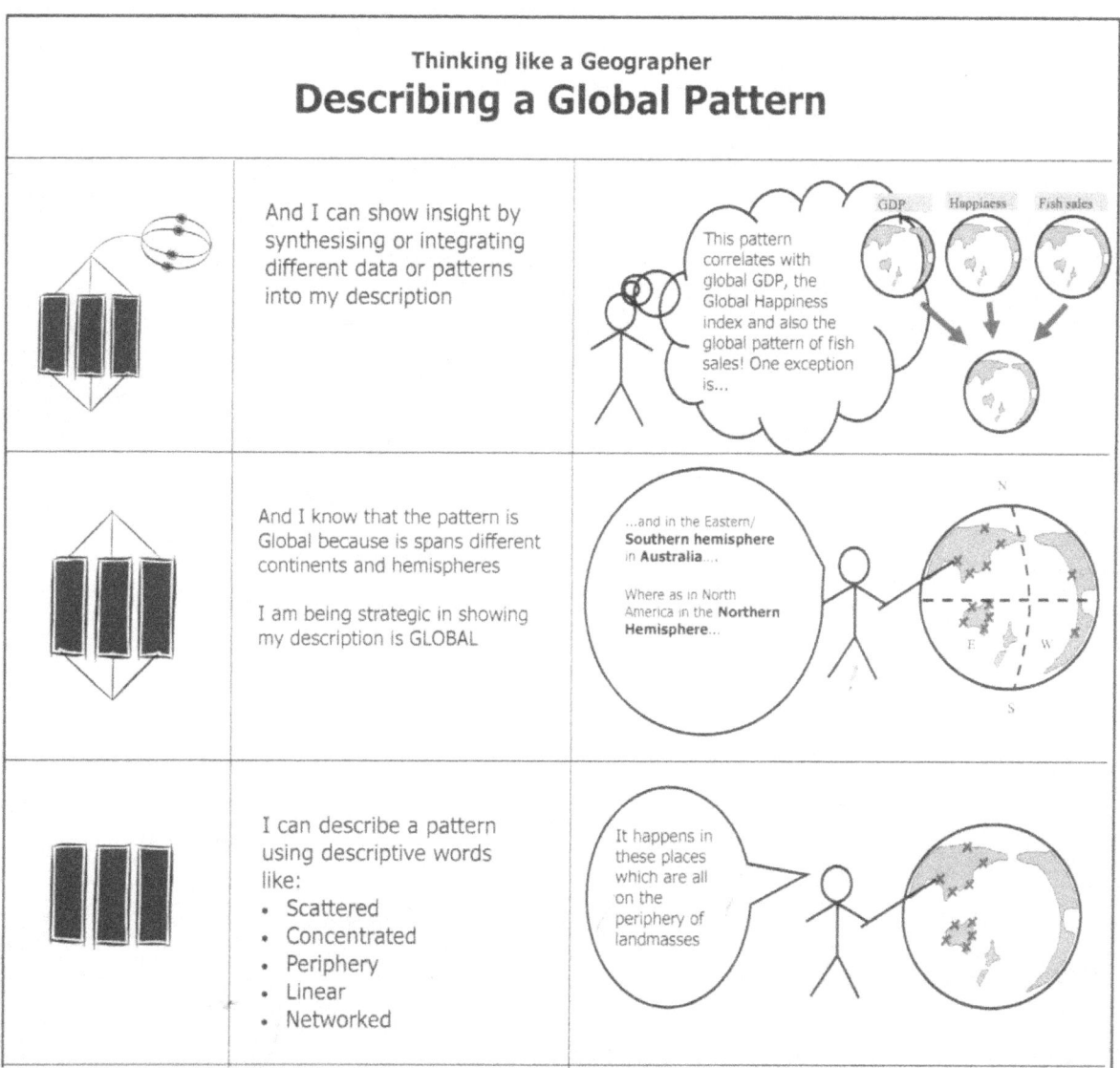

Exhibit 4.2: HOT SOLO Describe self-assessment visual rubric for describing how and why people use the environment

Describing how and why people use the environment

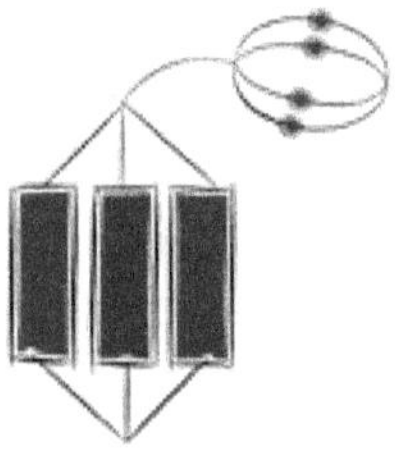	...and I can link it to a big idea or concept.	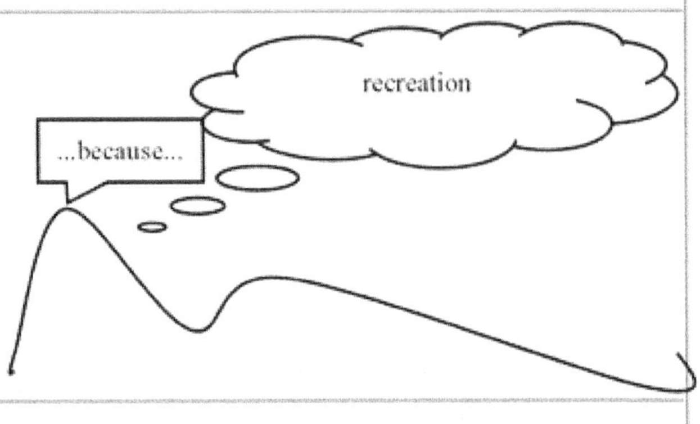 recreation ...because...
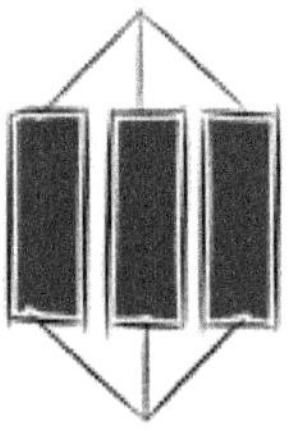	...and I can explain why they use the environment	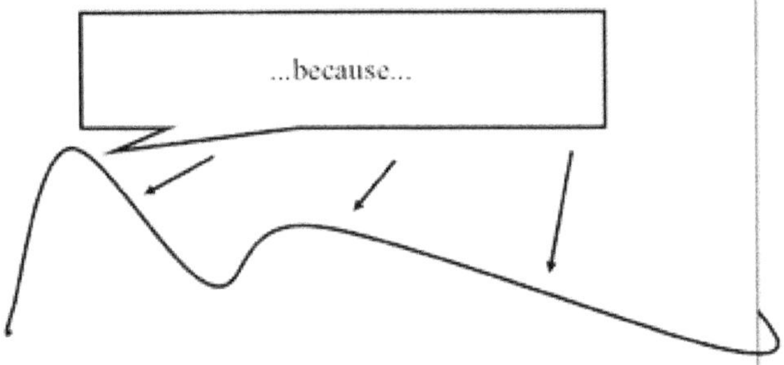 ...because...
	I can describe several ways that different people use the environment.	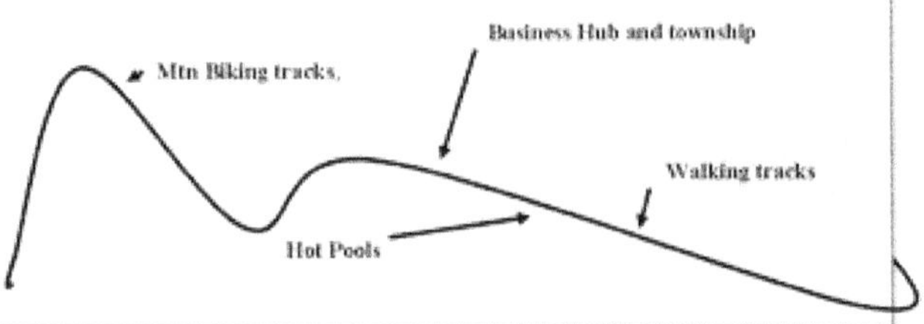 Mtn Biking tracks, Business Hub and township, Walking tracks, Hot Pools
	I can describe one use of the environment and why it is used for that purpose.	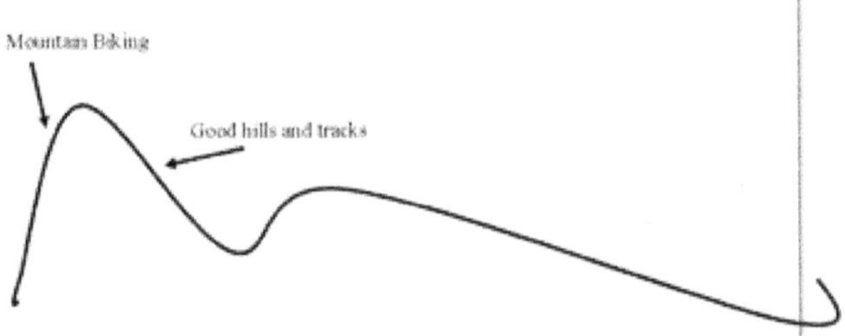 Mountain Biking, Good hills and tracks
	I have no idea...	 ?

My current level for _____ is _____. I say this because ....

My next step for improvement is ....

© Miriam Marshall Lincoln High School 2015 All rights reserved. Symbols used with permission HookED Pam Hook

Source: Miriam Marshall, Lincoln High School

Constructing resources

The following SOLO self-assessment rubric can be used to draw a précis sketch or map to explain social phenomena (Exhibit 4.3).

Exhibit 4.3: SOLO self-assessment visual rubric for drawing a précis sketch or map

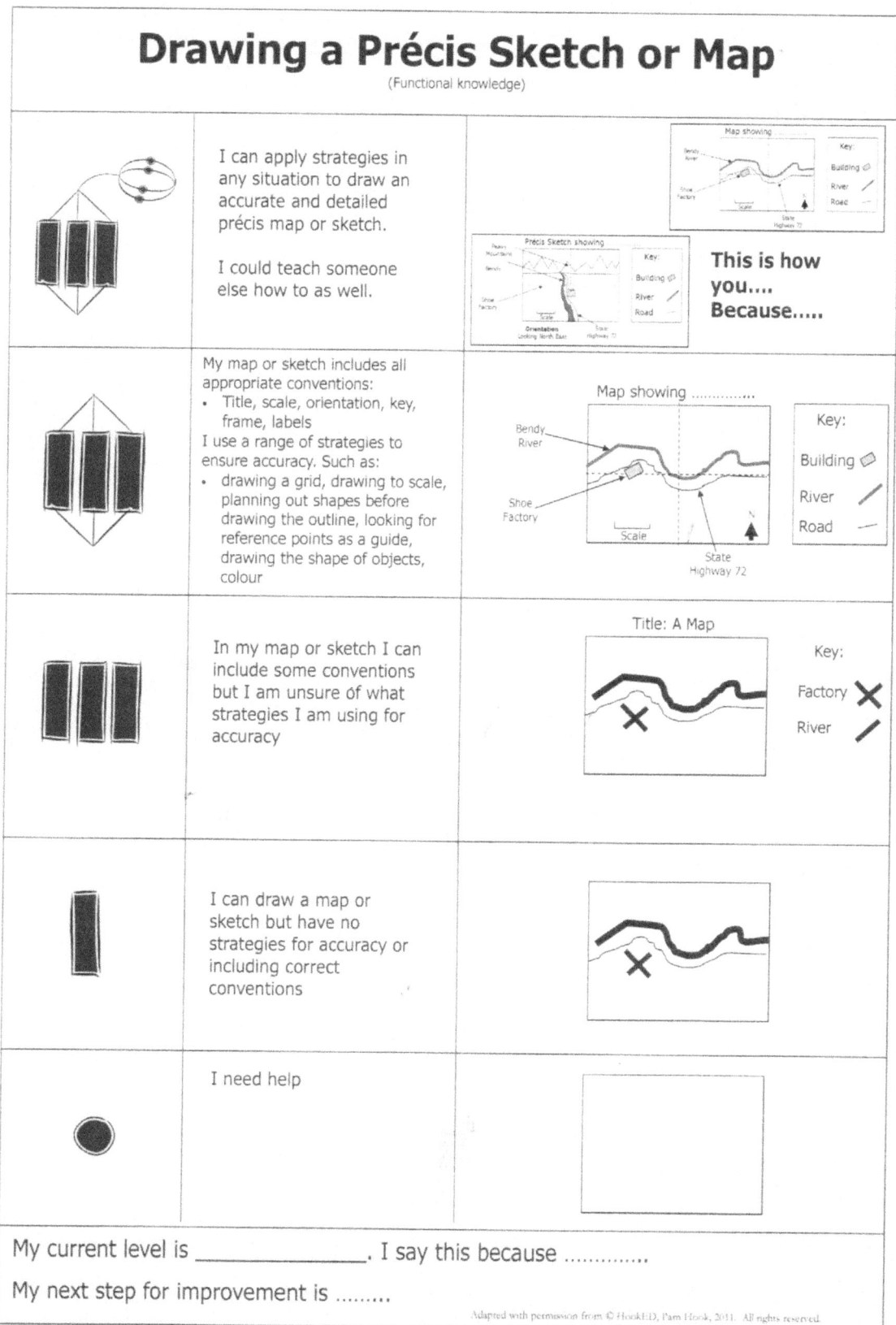

Communication skills

The following SOLO self-assessment rubrics support students in developing their communication skills through:

- writing a paragraph or essay (Exhibit 4.4)
- applying visuals to written work (Exhibit 4.5).

Exhibit 4.4: SOLO self-assessment visual rubric for writing a paragraph or essay

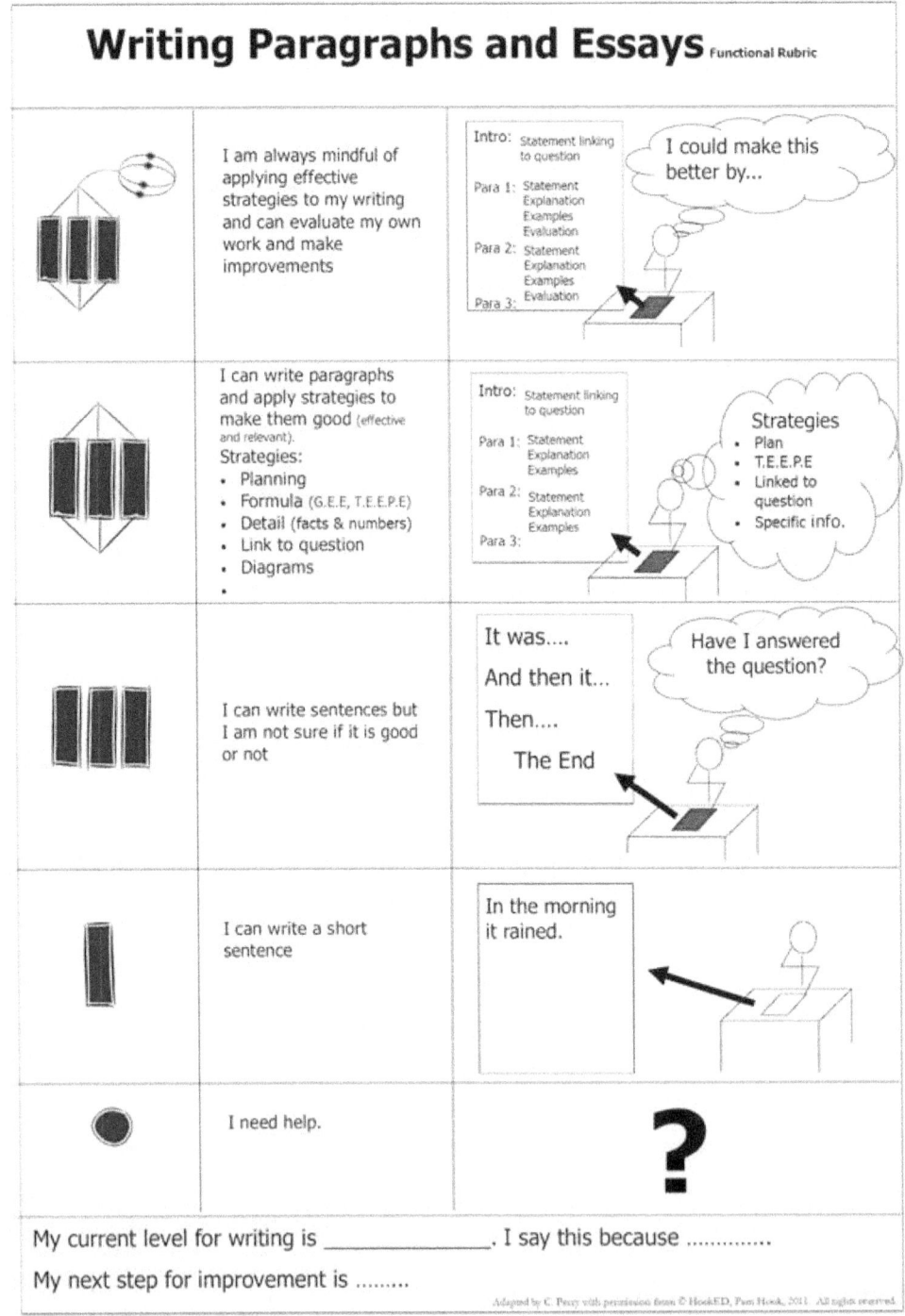

Exhibit 4.5: SOLO self-assessment rubric for applying visuals to written work

Learning goal: To explain why people want to use the environment

How do you get the coal out of the ground? What processes might you use? Make an annotated sketch of the next slide and show how you would mine/extract the coal. Use the self-assessment rubric to assess your annotation.

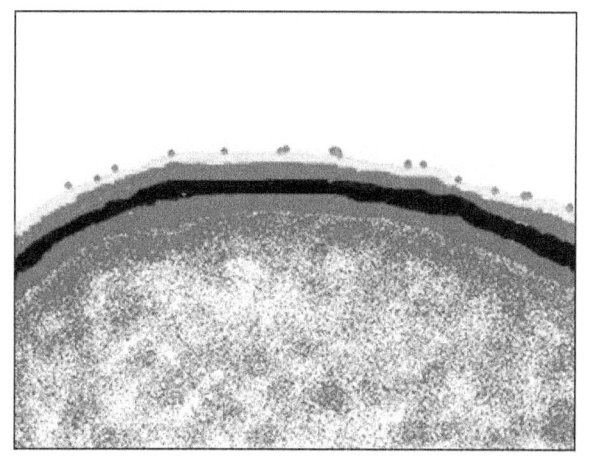
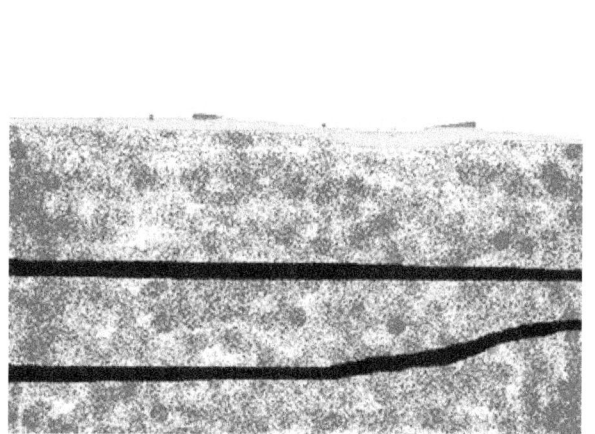

Annotating is a really important skill for the exams and assessments, so ...

How good is my "annotation"?

	I explain the process so well that if you had a digger, you could use my instructions and start work imediately
	I annotated a number of things and it explains the process I made valid links
	I annotated a number of things
	I annotated one thing
	I need help

Social skills

One of the goals of teaching social sciences is to develop action competence or student agency. The following SOLO self-assessment rubrics illustrate how we might make this process visible to students through:

- a visual map for demonstrating social action (Exhibit 4.6)
- a writing-based map for reporting on personal involvement in a social justice and human rights action (Exhibit 4.7).

Exhibit 4.6: SOLO self-assessment visual rubric for demonstrating social action

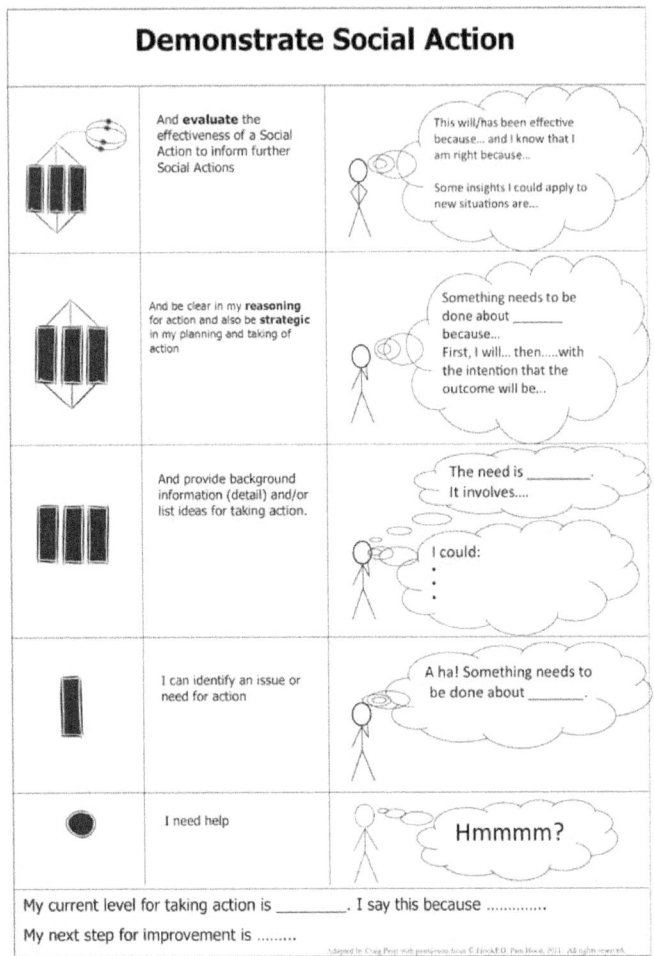

Exhibit 4.7: SOLO self-assessment rubric for reporting on personal involvement in a social justice and human rights action

	Multistructural	**Relational**	**Extended abstract**
• Describe • Explain and evaluate • Reflect and evaluate	My report describes: • the issue • what we aimed to do • what we did • how what we did promotes social justice and human rights. My report uses social studies concepts …	… **and** my report: • explains personal reasons for my involvement • evaluates the effectiveness of my personal involvement (effort and strategies).	… **and** my report: • reflects on alternative and/or additional actions • evaluates the potential effectiveness of these alternative and/or additional actions.
Effective strategies	• HookED SOLO Describe ++ map and self-assessment rubric • SOLO hexagons and reverse hexagons • Log of involvement • Visual evidence	• HOT SOLO Explain causes map and self-assessment rubric • SOLO functioning knowledge rubric for participation • Log of involvement • Visual evidence (photos)	• Brainstorming • Future problem-solving category list • SOLO hexagons • HOT SOLO Generalise map and self-assessment rubric • Criteria reference grid (Which is best?) • Diamond game ranking order activity

Fieldwork skills

Field sketches provide a record of observations and measurements taken in the field. By noting geological and/or structural features or annotating details likely to be missed in photographs, students develop an overall impression of the location of the social phenomenon under study. Exhibit 4.8 presents a SOLO self-assessment rubric for drawing a field sketch to help inform a community about a proposed future resource for their area.

Finally, Exhibit 4.9 sets out a SOLO self-assessment rubric for creating a survey about a social phenomenon. Although many online tools (eg, Google Forms in Google Drive or SurveyMonkey) provide some support with this task, creating a reliable and valid survey instrument is still not easy. It is often helpful to spend some time teaching students how to design a survey, unpacking flawed surveys and survey questions and co-constructing success criteria before students start to design their own surveys.

Exhibit 4.8: SOLO self-assessment visual rubric for drawing a field sketch about a proposed future resource

Draw a field sketch	
Extended abstract: I can seek feedback on how to improve my field sketch so that it clarifies the different perspectives groups and individuals hold about the future plans for the area.	
Relational: I can create a field sketch and annotate the important geographical features. My annotations help explain why the features are important and give a sense of scale and direction.	*(field sketch with full annotations)*
Multistructural: I can create a field sketch but I am not sure if I have annotated the important geographical features	*(field sketch with partial annotations)*
Unistructural: I can create a field sketch if I follow directions or copy someone else's sketch.	*(basic field sketch)*
Prestructural: I cannot make a sketch showing geographical features of the area	I cannot sketch
My current level for drawing a field sketch is …. I say this because …. My next step for improvement is …	

Exhibit 4.9: SOLO self-assessment rubric for creating a survey about a social phenomenon

Design a survey about a social phenomenon	Prestructural	Unistructural	Multistructural	Relational	Extended abstract
I can design a survey that includes: • clear instructions • short and concise questions • single questions • unbiased questions • fixed response questions • open questions (new ideas) • completion tracking • participant thanks • collation of responses.	I need help to design a survey about a social phenomenon.	I can design a survey about a social phenomenon if I am prompted or directed.	I use several strategies to design a survey about a social phenomenon but I am not sure when and/or why to use them. *(trial and error – aware of strategies but not sure why or when to use them so makes mistakes)*	I use several strategies to design a survey about a social phenomenon and I know when and why to use them. *(strategic or purposeful use of strategies – knows why and when).*	I use several strategies to design a survey about a social phenomenon and I know when and why to use them. I can teach others to design a survey about a social phenomenon. I act as a role model for others to help them design a survey about a social phenomenon. I seek feedback on how to improve the way I design a survey about a social phenomenon.
Effective strategies [insert strategies suggested by students and teachers]					

5. What do students say?

Students enjoy the freedom and control that comes with having a model that helps them understand learning, what they are doing, how well it is going and what they should do next in social inquiry. For a video of students from Lincoln High School, New Zealand talking about how SOLO is useful in their learning at school, go to: **https://youtu.be/vnTQzoqHdiI**

Below are more nuanced responses to SOLO strategies that students shared in surveys, which asked them to reflect on their use of SOLO graphic organisers (maps and rubrics), SOLO visual rubrics and SOLO chunking of assessment tasks.

> Using the SOLO maps meant I had all the links I would need to make already planned out.

> The SOLO maps had a positive effect as it got me to understand more and how I can relate information together.

> The maps helped because it made it more clear how to lay things out and it made it easier to write assessments off them as well.

> Good to refer to the SOLO maps in an assessment. Stops you from getting off topic in an assessment. They help a lot in planning what you're trying to say and when coupled with evidence = good grades.

> Having the SOLO maps and rubrics helped because it meant we knew what we were supposed to do for Achieve, Merit and Excellence. It actually showed what I need to get the marks I wanted.

> It helped to make me understand what I have to do to show deeper understanding – and there were some good sentence starters in there as well.

The students identified "clarity", "knowing exactly what we had to do", "how to integrate ideas" and "achieving academic success" as outcomes of using SOLO strategies.

Template 5.1 offers one survey that can be used to gather this kind of feedback on SOLO strategies.

Template 5.1: Survey asking for student reflection on SOLO strategies

Success = Effort + Effective strategies
Over this year, I have challenged you all to "aim high" and strive for success. One of my approaches has been to use SOLO Taxonomy to make effective strategies for success visible to you. Some examples of these strategies have been: • written and visual rubrics for the topics we have done so that you will know what success will look like • graphic organisers and SOLO symbols that make learning visible when we are bringing in information, making links or showing insight or using information in a new way • chunking assessments so they were not all done in one big group at the end. To reflect on the effectiveness of these teaching interventions, I need your feedback. Please rate each of the following by ticking the box on the scale that best fits what you think. Then write your reflections in the comments box.

1. SOLO visual rubrics to clarify what success (the standard) looks like and sounds like

Example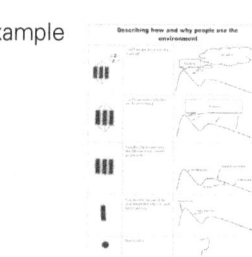

Definite negative effect	Some negative effect	No noticeable effect	Some positive effect	Definite positive effect

continued ...

© Essential Resources Educational Publishers Ltd

Template 5.1: Survey asking for student reflection on SOLO strategies (continued)

Comment/reasoning

2. SOLO graphic organisers to clarify levels of thinking and make links

   Examples

Definite negative effect	Some negative effect	No noticeable effect	Some positive effect	Definite positive effect

Comment/reasoning

3. Chunking assessment and using visual rubrics

Definite negative effect	Some negative effect	No noticeable effect	Some positive effect	Definite positive effect

Comment/reasoning

4. Any other comments or wonderings

Conclusions

[SOLO] made us very clear where we were going and, instead of just telling us what we had to do, it gave us lines of thought to go on. Student, Lincoln High School

SOLO Taxonomy is a model of learning that makes the surface and deep understandings of social inquiry visible to students and their teachers. As the examples in this book show, it can be used to enhance both teaching and learning in the social sciences. SOLO makes deep learning visible through a common language of learning about functioning and declarative knowledge outcomes as students learn to think like social scientists.

We have shared the many and various ways social sciences teachers and their students use SOLO in teaching and learning. The many SOLO strategies, templates, maps and rubrics in this book are accompanied by rich examples of work and comments from students. These examples show that SOLO brings clarity, detail and meaning to social inquiry, to the social sciences Best Evidence Synthesis (alignment, connection and community), and to declarative and functioning knowledge outcomes in the social sciences.

We hope the examples in this book will encourage you to share SOLO with your students so that they may learn to think like social scientists exploring social phenomena in skilled and active ways. SOLO fuels students and educators with curiosity, wondering, perspectives and insight about the world they live in now and how it may have differed in the past and may differ in the future.

References

Aitken, G and Sinnema, C. (2008) *Effective Pedagogy in Social Sciences: Tikanga ā Iwi: Best Evidence Synthesis.* URL: www.educationcounts.govt.nz/publications/series/2515/32879/35263

Biggs, J and Collis, K. (1982). *Evaluating the Quality of Learning: The SOLO Taxonomy.* New York: Academic Press.

Biggs, J. (1999). What the student does: teaching for enhanced learning. *Higher Education Research & Development* 18(1): 57–75.

Biggs, J and Tang, C. (2007). *Teaching for Quality Learning at University: What the student does* (3rd ed).Berkshire: Society for Research into Higher Education & Open University Press.

Goodman, MK. (2008). "Did Ronald McDonald also tend to scare you as a child?": working to emplace consumption, commodities, and citizen-students in a large classroom setting. *Journal of Geography in Higher Education* 32(3): 365–386.

Hayward, B. (2012). *Children, Citizenship and Environment: Nurturing a democratic imagination in a changing world.* London: Earthscan/Routledge

Hodgson, AM. (1992). Hexagons for systems thinking. *European Journal of Systems Dynamics* 59(1): 220–30.

Hook, P. (2015). *First Steps with SOLO Taxonomy. Applying the model in your classroom.* Invercargill: Essential Resources Educational Publishers Limited.

Hook, P and Cassé, B. (2013). *SOLO Taxonomy in the Early Years. Making connections for belonging, being and becoming.* Invercargill: Essential Resources Educational Publishers Limited.

Hook, P and Mills, J. (2011). *SOLO Taxonomy: A Guide for Schools. Book 1. A common language of learning.* Invercargill: Essential Resources Educational Publishers Limited.

Ministry of Education. (2007). *The New Zealand Curriculum: The English-medium teaching and learning in years 1–13.* Wellington: Learning Media.

Ministry of Education. (2008). *Approaches to Social Inquiry: Building conceptual understandings in the social sciences.* Wellington: Learning Media.

Ostler, A. (2011). 10 reasons why we need social science. Campaign for Social Science website.
URL: https://campaignforsocialscience.org.uk/news/10-reasons-why-you-need-social-science

Index of exhibits and templates

Exhibits

Constructive alignment in overview (Exhibit 2.4)	19
Example of student outcome using HookED SOLO reverse hexagons (Exhibit 2.15)	33
Examples of thinking strategies and e-learning differentiated against SOLO levels (Exhibit 2.11)	24
Higher-order thinking and SOLO Taxonomy (Exhibit 1.2)	7
HOT SOLO Describe self-assessment visual rubric for describing a global pattern (Exhibit 4.1)	55
HOT SOLO Describe self-assessment visual rubric for describing how and why people use the environment (Exhibit 4.2)	56
How we understand social phenomena (Exhibit 2)	5
Ostler's 10 reasons for studying the social sciences (Exhibit 1)	4
Overview of HOT and HookED maps linked to SOLO Taxonomy (Exhibit 2.12)	25
Skills and supporting SOLO strategies in a descriptive analysis (Exhibit 3.1)	37
SOLO declarative knowledge verbs aligned to differentiated learning activities (Exhibit 2.5)	20
SOLO-differentiated task sheet (Exhibit 2.7)	21
SOLO levels and NCEA achievement criteria applied to learning outcomes for "Explain a large natural environment" (Exhibit 2.9)	22
SOLO levels, symbols and hand signs (Exhibit 1.1)	6
SOLO Perspectives map for clarifying and scaffolding student thinking about perspectives (Exhibit 3.9)	52
SOLO Points of view and values questions and map focusing on early European settlement in New Zealand (Exhibit 3.8)	51
SOLO Points of view questions and map focusing on early European settlement in New Zealand (Exhibit 3.7)	50
SOLO self-assessment rubric for applying visuals to written work (Exhibit 4.5)	59
SOLO self-assessment rubric for building a learning community (knowing how to) (Exhibit 2.16)	35
SOLO self-assessment rubric for creating a survey about a social phenomenon (Exhibit 4.9)	62
SOLO self-assessment rubric for declarative knowledge (Exhibit 1.4)	8
SOLO self-assessment rubric for exploring values and perspectives (relational task) (Exhibit 1.10)	13
SOLO self-assessment rubric for finding out information (multistructural task) (Exhibit 1.8)	11
SOLO self-assessment rubric for functioning knowledge (Exhibit 1.3)	7
SOLO self-assessment rubric for identifying the focus of the learning (relational/extended abstract task) (Exhibit 1.6)	10
SOLO self-assessment rubric for outcomes from the SOLO-differentiated task sheet (Exhibit 2.8)	22
SOLO self-assessment rubric for reflecting and evaluating (extended abstract task) (Exhibit 1.7)	11
SOLO self-assessment rubric for reporting on personal involvement in a social justice and human rights action (Exhibit 4.7)	60
SOLO self-assessment visual rubric for demonstrating social action (Exhibit 4.6)	60
SOLO self-assessment visual rubric for drawing a field sketch about a proposed future resource (Exhibit 4.8)	61
SOLO self-assessment visual rubric for drawing a précis sketch or map (Exhibit 4.3)	57
SOLO self-assessment visual rubric for generalising based on insight (Exhibit 3.10)	53

SOLO self-assessment visual rubric for writing a paragraph or essay (Exhibit 4.4)	58
SOLO strategies to support the separate tasks that contribute to finding insight (Exhibit 3.11)	54
SOLO Taxonomy levels apply throughout the social inquiry process (Exhibit 1.5)	10
Student example of using a HOT SOLO Predict map to make predictions about Japanese cars (Exhibit 3.4)	43
Student example of using a SOLO Integrate concepts map to develop conceptual thinking (Exhibit 3.6)	47
Student examples of writing a prediction with and without the scaffolding of the HOT SOLO Predict map (Exhibit 3.5)	44
Student pointing to the level of learning outcome on a SOLO self-assessment visual rubric (Exhibit 2.1)	16
Student use of a HookED SOLO Describe ++ map to describe a social action (Exhibit 3.2)	37
Student use of a HookED SOLO Explain causes map to explain the causes of Japanese youth cultures (Exhibit 3.3)	40
Student work sample for explaining viewpoints (extended abstract outcome) (Exhibit 1.11)	14
Student work sample for gathering information and identifying sources (extended abstract outcome) (Exhibit 1.9)	12
Student's reflection on level of knowing before and after a task on explaining Japanese youth culture (Exhibit 2.3)	19
Using SOLO "plus 1 " to relate the level of prior knowledge to an appropriate next step (Exhibit 2.6)	21
Using SOLO hexagons to determine prior knowledge (Exhibit 2.2)	17
Using SOLO strategies to think deeply about the effect of European settlers on indigenous people (Exhibit 2.14)	28–29
Using the HookED SOLO Learning Intention Generator and SOLO verbs to create tasks of increasing cognitive complexity (Exhibit 2.10)	23
Writing a generalisation about "Why people use the Stockton Plateau for mining" (Exhibit 2.13)	26–27

Templates

HookED SOLO Describe ++ map (Template 3.1)	38
HookED SOLO Describe ++ self-assessment rubric (Template 3.2)	39
HookED SOLO Explain causes map (Template 3.3)	41
HookED SOLO Explain causes self-assessment rubric (Template 3.4)	42
HookED SOLO reverse hexagons (Template 2.4)	32
HOT SOLO Compare and contrast map (Template 2.2)	30
HOT SOLO Compare and contrast self-assessment rubric (Template 2.3)	31
HOT SOLO Generalise map (Template 3.7)	48
HOT SOLO Generalise self-assessment rubric (Template 3.8)	49
HOT SOLO Predict map (Template 3.5)	45
HOT SOLO Predict self-assessment rubric (Template 3.6)	46
SOLO learning log and self-assessment rubric to determine prior knowledge and next steps (Template 2.1)	18
Survey asking for student reflection on SOLO strategies (Template 5.1)	63–64

www.ingramcontent.com/pod-product-compliance
Lightning Source LLC
Chambersburg PA
CBHW080046230426
43672CB00014B/2832